Robert Paton

The Scottish Church and Its Surroundings

In early times

Robert Paton

The Scottish Church and Its Surroundings
In early times

ISBN/EAN: 9783337191948

Printed in Europe, USA, Canada, Australia, Japan

Cover: Foto ©Lupo / pixelio.de

More available books at **www.hansebooks.com**

THE

SCOTTISH CHURCH

AND

ITS SURROUNDINGS,

IN EARLY TIMES.

BY

ROBERT PATON,

MINISTER OF KIRKINNER.

EDINBURGH: JAMES GEMMELL.

1884.

PREFACE.

THE following sketches contain, in a more or less
connected form, a bird's-eye view of the rise and
development of Christianity in Britain, especially
North Britain, during the first seven centuries of our
era. They were first delivered to the congregation
and parishioners of Kirkinner, and formed a course
of monthly lectures in the winters of 1881-1882,
1882-1883. The aim the writer had in view in their
construction was, to exhibit in a popular form the
rise and progress of the Church in connection with
the general history of our country in these early
times. In carrying out this object, occasional side-
lights have been borrowed from the "world's broad
pavement," and contemporary events and movements
in that wider sphere have been explained and illus-
trated, rather than simply alluded to, that those to
whom such researches are unfamiliar may be the

better able to understand the subject, at least in a general way. As the authorities founded on are sufficiently indicated in the body of this work, it will not be necessary to particularise here on the matter further than to say that the author has adopted generally the view of Skene in regarding the Picts, as well as the Scots, as a Gaelic speaking people; while the use made in these pages of Fuller, characterised by Coleridge as one who, "next to Shakespeare," excited in him "the sense and emotion of the marvellous," has been simply to clothe in that writer's felicitous and quaint literary style facts otherwise abundantly verified. The feeling that, in our retrospect, we are too apt to stop short at the Reformation, and that an appearance of haste in slipping over pre-Reformation epochs has characterised some, if not all, of our more elaborate treatises on Scottish Church History, has in some measure determined the author to indulge in a quiet and leisurely stroll among these early and unfamiliar walks. The period embraced in these pages, from the earliest ages to the end of the 7th century, gives us the dawn of Christianity on the background of heathen darkness; the few drops ushering in the shower of blessing that came to our land with the advent of Christianity,—the rise and progress of the Celtic Church, first in South Britain, then in the north under Columba and his monks,—the progress of Culdee missionary enterprise till the time of Bede, when it had reached its zenith. This, which forms a distinct epoch in the evolution of our Scottish Christianity, is interesting not merely as a portion of our past history, but as containing within it the embryo of those distinctive features which, when the Reformation wave passed over us, crystallized in the north into Presbytery, while in the South Christianity emerged in Episcopalian forms.

The qualifications necessary for the treatment of historical subjects are by no means universally distributed, and in no case can they be attained without a considerable expenditure of labour. To be able to " transcend the special limitations of his time ;" to exhibit a fullness and thoroughness of knowledge, never failing at any point over the whole field ; to lift the story up, and make it lucid by general points of view ; to throw the whole into historical perspective with suggestive background, are conditions which require to be satisfied by the historian.

To recognise that it is possible so to manage correct

knowledge as to leave a strikingly incorrect impression;—so to group events together in crowded chapters that one "cannot see the wood for the trees;"—so to sink from a position of commanding survey as to drag the story along in the hollow of events, and treat all as on the same level, is a qualification no less necessary than the foregoing. But the ecclesiastical historian must, in addition, have a special eye to the operation of the greatest force at work in human affairs, and exhibit Christianity in the deep sky of social evolution—in the relation of "organism" and "environment." How far the author of the following pages has failed to reach such an ideal he himself is deeply conscious; but if their perusal shall give the reader as much pleasure as he has experienced in their construction, and stimulate to fresh interest in that department of our national history in which lies our true glory, he will conceive himself amply rewarded. R. P.

THE MANSE, KIRKINNER,
October, 1883.

CONTENTS.

CHAPTER   PAGE

I. Introduction—The Druids—St. Ninian—Shrine of
St. Ninian, ... 1

II. Druidism — Paganism— Christianity — Our Celtic
Ancestors, ... 9

III. The Darkness and the Dawn—The Roman Occupation—First British Evangelists—Boadicea, . 15

IV. Lucius, "a Nursing Father"—Christianity Extending—Persecution—The first Christian Emperor, 24

V. Nature Worship—Heroic Mythology—Christianity
and Heretical Blends—Socinianism—Sabellianism—Arianism—Pelagianism, . . . 31

VI. Caledonia " Stern and Wild" –Chaos and Darkness
— Saxon Invasion — Pelagian Controversy —
" Alleuiatic Victory "—Palladius—St. Patrick—
St. Ninian—Columba, . . 43

VII. Columba—Asceticism—Monachism—Simeon the
Stylite—St. Anthony—Literary Labours of the
Monks, ... 60

VIII. Life of Columba—Ireland's Golden Age—Ancient
Ecclesiastical Buildings — Discipline, Training,
and Labours of the Culdees—Columba's Evangelistic Labours—Visits St. Kentigern—his death, 74

CHAPTER   PAGE

IX. Mediævalism—Picts and Scots—St. Kentigern—
his Austerities and Labours,   .   .   89

X. Early Modes of Evangelisation—Caledonia Regen-
erated, ...   100

XI. Mohammed and Gregory I.—The Crescent and the
Cross—The good Missionary Pope—Augustine's
Mission to England—Rome and Iona meet in
England, ...   105

XII. Edwin, King of Northumberland—Christianity in
Conflict with Heathenism—Edwin's Conversion
to Christianity—The good King Oswald—Oswald
and Aidan—Brother Oswald,   .   .   117

XIII. Rise of the Papal Power—Gregory the Great no
Papist — Presbytery and Prelacy — Heretical
Popes—Rome and Iona—Synod of Whitby,   .   130

XIV. Conclusion—The Abbess Hilda—The Poet Cædmon—St. Cuthbert—The Venerable Bede,   143

THE SCOTTISH CHURCH AND ITS SURROUNDINGS.

CHAPTER I.

INTRODUCTION :—THE DRUIDS—ST. NINIAN—SHRINE OF
ST. NINIAN.

THE dawn and early development of Christianity in Britain, especially in the north; its general and special aspects; the forms it assumed; and the phases it passed through, is the subject of this course of lectures. It is a large subject, and cannot be adequately treated in this way—all that can be done is to present to the reader a few of the leading features which characterised the origin and progress of Christianity in this land—to obtain some glimpses into the early condition of our religion, out of which our present condition has been formed. It is a difficult subject; to walk in the dark corridors of the past, where the dimmest outline of objects is sometimes all that can be seen, to find one after another of the lights in the path to be only of the Will-o'-the-Wisp order.

Yet when we consider the importance of the subject, and the interest with which it is invested, belonging to that past out of which the brightest features of our present have been moulded, our attempts, however inadequate and imperfect, to pierce the gloom and haze that envelopes it may not be altogether futile. To map out and trace to their varied sources the different theological currents in which Christianity has at different points touched our shores. To define the various embryo forms out of which our present ecclesiastical institutions have been developed, cannot in any way be fully treated. A few broad facts which stand out in bold relief, which will serve as landmarks to the general situation, must suffice. Paganism in its Druidic form ; Christianity embodied in Celtic, Anglo-Norman, and Romanised forms, are the broad, general features of our religious history from the days of Julius Cæsar to the era of John Knox. How long our ancestors had sat under the shadow of heathen darkness, and through what forms of superstition they had passed before the Roman power touched our shores, belongs to a wild and trackless region of conjecture. Imagination, that "licensed trespasser, that climbs over walls and peeps in at windows," points out Phœnician ships, manned by Baal worshippers, laden with merchandise, sailing along the shores of the Mediterranean sea, gliding past the Iberian coast, and at some periods, between the time of Solomon and that of the Roman Conquest of Britain, touching our Cornish shores, and inoculating the land with the

worship of the great sun-god Baal, which, filtering in
the dark Celtic mind, through the lapse of time,
appears in the form of the Druid superstition as that
system was seen by Julius Cæsar and Pliny. Over
the process of assimilation and growth, under which
the religion of Ahab's wife became thus transmuted,
an awful darkness reigns. When the Romans lift up
the curtain and give us a peep at what is going on
in this land 1800 years ago, we see Pagan priests,
under the shadow of the oak tree whereon the misle-
toe grew, invocating their gods, and, on the sixth day
of the moon, at the beginning of their year, offering
white bulls, filleted in the horns, amid many ceremonies. As to what is in their heads in the shape of
theological belief, we are left in ignorance. For, as
Fuller quaintly remarks—"Those Pagan priests never
wrote anything, so as to procure the greater veneration to their mysteries; men being bound to believe
that it was some great treasure that was locked up in
such great secrecy." All we know with certainty is,
as the learned Pliny informs us, that "they were great
magicians; insomuch that the very Persians, in some
sort, might seem to have learned their magic from the
Britons." If the Roman superstition ever effected an
entrance into this part of Britain, and coated over the
older Druidic system, it must have been as a mere film
which gave way to the slightest wear and tear. Any
faint traces of it that may exist are altogether over-
shadowed by the numerous monuments of the Druid
superstition that still exist. In the south of Britain

Apollo and Diana were worshipped by those who formerly were Druids. Especially was Diana a favourite object of worship at a time when Britain was one great hunting forest. "There is a place near St. Paul's, in London," says Fuller, "called in old records 'Diana's Chamber,' where, in the days of King Edward I., thousands of the heads of oxen were digged up which were the proper sacrifices to Diana, whose great temple was built thereabout." But while in England the Roman Paganism forms thus one distinct phase through which religious thought passed in early times, there is no reason to believe that that system in this northern region ever gained sufficient influence to displace the aboriginal superstition. In South Britain they gave up one lie and accepted another in its stead—they gave up the Druid lie and accepted the Roman lie. But our ancestors were more Conservative in their action, they stuck to the old lie till they found the truth. Druidism they retained till it was finally shouldered out by Christianity. Druidism was the "strong man armed," but Christianity was the "stronger." Before the conversion of the Picts and Scots to Christianity, they seem to have been in a very benighted state. All reliable accounts represent them as being a very savage race, as being to a large extent made up of the animal, even the wild animal, element. Gildas, the earliest of our historians, speaks of them as a race "who were more eager to shroud their villainous faces in bushy hair than to cover their bodies with decent clothing." When the first rays of

Christian light gleamed on our northern shores, whither it was perhaps carried by those Roman legions, that may have listened to the preaching of Paul in Rome, it would seem as if "the darkness comprehended it not;" but it is satisfactory to learn that, as early as the second century, the light that first broke over the mountains of Judea lighted up, though in fitful flashes, our northern sky. Swathed in the mists of legend and fable, we see Christianity like an abnormal fact dropped into the stream of our national life.

Surrounded by a halo of light there stands in front of the darkness, St Ninian, a man of Apostolic fervour. He sees with clear-sighted vision the demands of the age. In the fourth century—when the Church was first established under Constantine—when St. Martin of Tours (whose Christian excellence is annually brought to mind at the winter term called by his name) introduced monachism into the west, when the Goths and Huns were swarming at the very gates of the seat of Empire, just before the Roman legions were called home to the defence of Italy, there was established at Whithorn, by St. Ninian, the celebrated Candida Casa, the first stone edifice erected in this country for the worship of God. St. Ninian stands before us as a hero, a God-gifted man, the apostle of Scotland, as St. Patrick, his contemporary, was apostle of Ireland. Though not the first to sow Christian truth in the land, he was the first to sow it on a large scale. He appears as a great spiritual captain, who dispersed the forces of darkness by the power of divine truth. He has some rough work to do, ploughing and harrowing over a hard paganised soil, but he advances steadily, preaching the gospel, not here and there, but over the length and breadth of the land, from Whithorn in the south to the Grampians in the north. The venerable Bede calls him "this most reverend bishop and holy man of the British nation." The Roman power triumphed over the southern parts of Britain, where they sowed the seeds of the old pagan civilisation, but St. Ninian obtained more glorious triumphs when he converted the Southern Picts in this country from heathen darkness to Christian light, and sowed the "good seed" of the word broadcast over the land. The Romans left monuments behind them in walls and bridges, and theatres, and palaces, but in Candida Casa we have a monument which speaks to the ages of a work more glorious by far than that represented by all the memorials of ancient Rome. It speaks of conquests won in the conversion of heathen tribes who had resisted all the efforts of the Roman arms, and who had been the terror of the Britons in the south. To Whithorn, then, we look for the first Christian shrine, whence emanated the great light that first dispelled paganism on a large scale from the land. And when, in the lapse of time, St. Ninian had gone to his rest, and all those apostolic men who were his coadjutors in the great work had passed away, that light flickered and faded there only to burst forth elsewhere in

greater effulgence. We have no direct means of ascer-
taining the results of St. Ninian's labours; but if we
may judge from the halo of glory that tradition has
shed round his memory, these must have been of the
most satisfactory character. In the following note,
appended to "Murray's Literary History of Galloway,"
we have a succinct account of the traditional aspects
in which his life has been enbalmed and handed down
to our day:—"There is not a saint in the Romish
Calendar whose memory was more venerated, and
whose tomb was oftener visited, than those of Ninian.
In Galloway, until this day, his name is familiar as
'household words,' even with the most illiterate of the
people. A cave on the sea coast, about two miles
from Whithorn, to which, amid the intervals of his
holy labours, he occasionally retired, is still pointed
out with something like superstitious awe and veneration; and traditions respecting his supposed miracles,
and his holiness, are told and cherished with a degree
of reverence and credulity to which almost no other
district can produce a parallel. Several places and
parishes, both in England and in Scotland, bear his
name. Crowds of pilgrims, for many ages, annually
resorted to his shrine—even some of our Scottish
monarchs have visited it. The Queen of James III.
undertook this pilgrimage in 1474; and in 1507 James
IV. made the same pilgrimage *on foot*, to pray for the
health and recovery of his Queen, who had been alarm-
ingly ill in child-bed; to testify his resignation to the
death of his two infant children; and to express his

penitence for having rebelled against his father." In the absence of contemporary accounts of the saint's career in evangelising this country, we have only to penetrate beneath the surface of those legends and traditions in which his memory is preserved, to recognise in him whose shrine was the attraction of pilgrims from all parts for 1000 years, a prince and a great man who left his mark in this country—an evangelist who, with the torch of the Gospel, went about among our heathen ancestors, lighting up their darkness. The marvels ascribed to him by tradition may well be set aside as myths; and which, even if true, are incomparably inferior to the one grand miracle by which he triumphed over Heathenism in our land, not by one stupendous blow, but rather by inserting the thin end of the wedge of Christianity, which was to prepare the way for the ultimate overthrow of the Druid Superstition.

CHAPTER II.

IN my last lecture, I presented you with a brief
outline of the field to be covered by these
sketches. I propose now to begin to fill in
the details, by first of all taking a bird's-eye view of
the conditions and environment of Christianity in
the early dawn of its existence in this country. As
an adequate knowledge of this subject can only be
attained by a process of diving below the surface and
discovering the original foundations, I shall endea-
vour to trace the rise and progress of Christianity in
this land on the background of the social and political
conditions in which it first appears like a rainbow in
the darkness. As it was during the Roman occupation of this country that the seeds of Christianity and
civilisation were sown in British soil, a passing glance
at the circumstances in which that power came to be
established in Britain will first engage our attention.
And as the Celtic Church, the parent Church of
Britain, which afterwards dominated in the north for
500 years, did not see the light in this part of Britan
till after it had passed through a chequered career in
the south, our attention at present will be devoted

more particularly to South Britain, where we see the
embryo of the Celtic Church exhibiting Christianity
at first in a vague neutrality of tint, struggling for
existence between the two fires of Paganism and
Druidism, to be afterwards rudely shaken and well-
nigh extinguished by the subsequent advent of Thor
and Woden. What may be described as the secular
basis of this subject, the first topic to be here treated,
will not be considered out of place by any competent
student of sociology, while the Christian, who recog-
nises the hand of God in the disposal of all things,
will, in the series of events which led up to the establishment of Christianity in this land, see in miniature
a typical illustration of those wider movements in the
world which prepared the way for the advent of the
Redeemer. Little, indeed, would be gained by notic-
ing the introduction of so strange and supernatural a
factor as Christianity into our history, if the elements
in which that factor were to work did not constitute,
in the record, a strong foil to it by force of vivid
reality. What is aimed at is not merely to see Christianity dropped into the stream of our national existence; but, along with this, to keep a steady and
clear-sighted eye on the ordinary course and complexion of things, to behold with intense vision, the
effect on that course of something which transcends
and transfigures it into new forms and features. It
is to survey the character of the soil on which the
seed of the Word was to be sown, to note the interaction of the aboriginal superstition and the elegant

mythology of Pagan Rome ; to trace the advent of a power that was destined to triumph over both in a mighty spiritual conquest, in which Christianity assimilated to itself all the elements of vitality in either, and relegated to the lumber department of creation the dross of both. In this way we shall be led to trace to the vanishing point the old potent nature worship of the Druids in its retreat to the West, where, in the island of Anglesea, it cowered before the arms of the Pagan idolaters, when Apollo sat securely in what is now Westminster Abbey, and Diana was worshipped at St Paul's. We shall thus appear to see their dark vanishing shadows hovering for a little among things not realised as yet, but which had in them the promise and potency of all that has, during the last 1800 years, ennobled and elevated our State. We shall see, in fine, Christianity arising in its might on the ruins of the old mythologies, and the whole cloudland of ignorance and error melting before it in the issuing radiance of Divine truth.

The island of Britain was, during the Roman occupation, divided into three, and, at a later period, into five provinces, each with its respective metropolis. The part of the island that was never thus occupied extended from the Forth and Clyde, in the south, to the Pentland Firth, in the north. This region was called Caledonia, Alban, or Pictland, and was inhabited by a barbarous race of people called Picts, a colony of whom also occupied Galloway in that remote age. The south of the island was peopled by a number of

British tribes, while Ireland, then called Scotia, was the home of the Scots, who, however, early began to colonise the West Highlands of Scotland. The original inhabitants of these islands were the ancient Gauls or Celts, a branch of the primitive Aryan race—the family that had its home in central Asia at a time when things seem dim in the eyes of historians, "like reflected moonbeams on a distant lake." They were among the first who left their parent home in the East, in accordance with a general law of movement which has characterised the families of men from the earliest times. In the course of their migrations, these swarms from the parent hive carried fire and sword, confusion and desolation, everywhere. They were thorns in the side of the Roman power centuries before Christ, at which time they had overrun all Europe and Asia Minor. In the old Irish, the Highland Scotch, the Manx, and the Welsh, we have survivals, in affiliated dialects, of a language that, more than 2000 years ago, was spoken not only in Britain, but throughout the whole of Europe, and a considerable portion of Asia. At the dawn of our country's history, when the Romans invaded our shores, these Celtic hordes were grouped in tribes, or clans, or communities, more or less compactly organised. They lived in mud tents; they wore scarcely any clothes; they painted their bodies; they delighted in war, which they practised very freely on each other; they hunted the boar, the deer, the wolf. In canoes made out of hollow trees, or in boats made out of wicker work covered with skins, they navigated lake and sea. In civilisation they were advanced about as far as some African tribes and village communities of the present day. Only in the south-east portion of the island, which was colonised by the Belgæ before the time of Julius Cæsar, was agriculture carried on. Holding a high place among these ancient Britons was a class of men already mentioned as ministers of religion. They were named Druids. They presided at sacrifices; they instructed the young; they administered justice; they dwelt in groves, and taught in caves or forests; they offered human sacrifices. In all causes, both criminal and civil, their decision was final; and if any person, however eminent, refused to abide by their sentence, he was interdicted the public sacrifices, and treated as an outlaw; his society was shunned, and he was denied the common rights of a citizen. In short, their power was absolute; for, armed with the doctrine of metempsychosis, they carried their authority as far as the fears of the people. Their government was of the simplest patriarchal character, a large measure of liberty, and even lawlessness, occasionally disturbing the centre of gravity of the particular tribes; while what may be called their international or intertribal relations were not seldom characterised by broils and battles, in which boundaries and landmarks were constantly shifting their position, illustrating, in this respect, rather the mutability of human affairs than the repose and fixity of nature. Over this chaos of conflicting

interests and confusion of disturbed ownership the
Roman power spread its net of organised government
and law.   To trace the rise and progress of that dread
power that accomplished the conquest of Britain, to
contemplate the stealthy advances of that dominion,
which, beginning with a few tribes on the banks of
the Tiber, at length established a world-wide empire,
however interesting, would here be out of place.   All
that is necessary for the purpose of these sketches is
to take a brief survey of the process by which our
country was first brought within the influence of the
world's civilisation, redeemed from a position in which
it bore the most scanty relations to the great outside
world, and brought, by the social influence of the
Roman power, to a stage of development at which its
position could be settled in the " file " of contemporary
nations.   But for the Roman conquest, our country
must have continued in that state of Cimmerian darkness in which it then was, when the torch of civilisation revealed a state of things here which appears
like the figures that glide over the field of a camera
obscura—not an abiding fact in it all.

CHAPTER III.

WE now propose to note a few of the landmarks of our history at the period of the Roman invasion, viewing the story as the transparent medium through which the deeper life movements can be traced. "Every man," it has been well said, "reads nature by his own lamp." Our ancestors had read nature by their own lamp long enough— they required now the light of one that was brighter and more powerful, and that was supplied by the Roman power. The thoughts of these wild men, our savage ancestors, had long been shut up with their own inborn horrors, breathing choke-damp instead of mountain air, when the Romans led them out of the dark forest of their own imaginations to the world's broad pavement—the very highways of human culture. Something, then, required to be done—some shock of ruin to visit them, some door to be burst open, some roof to be blown away, some rock to be blasted, that light and air might have free access to their spiritual house, without which it could never grow stately. The call was clamant. The Roman power came, and came not a moment too soon. It broke through all barriers, the legions streamed in all directions through the land, their thoughts could not but establish also a right of way through the dark Celtic mind, leaving many a phantom conclusion behind, as a strong-minded man forces his way within the precincts of another's personality, leaving his own deposits there. The Romans came ; with one hand they held the sword, and with the other they scattered choicest treasures in our land. Wherever they went there was a silent, invisible power at work, breaking down the old chaos and establishing order in its stead. The living falsehood that, in the shape of the Druid mythology, had long walked and talked among our rude ancestors, was now doomed. The time was ready for its own new birth. The conscience, the intellect of the nation, was being awakened; flashes of moral electricity were passing in various directions through the chaotic mass. A want was being created which Roman culture could not satisfy. That culture exhibited life on a higher platform, and could have lifted our nation to a higher level of moral conviction than it had either attained, or was in the least likely to attain, of itself. Meanwhile some good, undefinable as the faint influences of starlight, soon began to appear from another quarter. It was not anything in Roman culture. It was something hidden in a deep cistern, which the Romans conveyed to our shores. They were the living acqueducts by which streams of living water were brought to our land fresh from the fountains of Judæa. Out of the misery of the grimy little cellar of their dark life, the heart's cry of our nation was for light, "true light," and life, "life more abundantly." He who is the living heart of the universe, with whom misery is as the voice of prayer, heard that cry, and was meanwhile guiding the chariot of the Roman power, sure as the flight of a comet, straight to His purpose. As Mount Sinai once resounded with the thunder of a visible presence, so, amid the noise and tumult and terrors of war, the advent of the Redeemer was heralded to our land, where the people "that sat in darkness" saw "great light." This tortured little world of human hearts cried aloud, as it were, for a Saviour, with unutterable groaning, and Heaven's answer came when the successors of Julius Cæsar first invaded our British shores. Half a century before Christ the Roman power was perceived by our ancestors arising as "a little cloud out of the sea, like a man's hand." A century later it overshadowed the whole land, from the shores of Kent and Cornwall to the Firths of Forth and Clyde. Before this was accomplished, before the hardy Britons were subdued, the force and discipline of the legions of Rome were subjected to many a shock, and not a few reverses, in the field. Wave after wave of Roman valour broke itself upon the cliff-like obstinacy of these rude Celtic warriors, who resisted the invaders at all points. But, from first to last, the superiority of Roman discipline left no doubt as to the event. From the time when Cassivelaunus faced the great Cæsar, only to be himself

B

peremptorily snuffed out, and his capital in a blaze
around him, to the defeat of Galgacus, who, with his
back to the Grampians and his face to the foe, fell on
the blood-stained field among his valiant Caledonians,
the history of the advances of the Roman power in
this land was characterised by scenes of blood and
strife, the forces of civilisation and barbarism in un-
equal conflict, the latter inevitably doomed to go to
the wall.

Two episodes in the history of this long campaign
I select for a moment's consideration here, the one
forming a probable clue to the earliest pioneers of
Christianity, while the other exhibits the expiring
agonies of Druidism in South Britain. In the reign
of Claudius, Caractacus, *alias* Caradoc, with his
Britons, went out to meet the advancing Romans,
who had penetrated into the country of the Silures (a
name immortalised by Sir R. J. Murchison in connection with the geological formation of its rocks), a warlike nation that inhabited the banks of the Severn.
Tacitus tells the story of the defeat of the Britons.
Their camp was stormed with great slaughter, though
not without considerable resistance. The wife and
daughter of Caractacus were taken prisoners to Rome.
The Senate was summoned together on the occasion
of their arrival. Many speeches were delivered, the
centre of interest being the invasion of Britain and
the capture of the British Prince, who, with his wife
and daughter and brothers, were made to pass before
the Emperor in view of the assembly. The picture

drawn of the valiant chief by the pen of the Roman historian is a graphic one. In the midst of that august assembly, the very focus of the world's civilisation, the fountain-head of its law and administration, there stood the savage chief, his body almost naked, and painted with figures of animals, with a chain of iron about his neck, and another about his middle, the hair of his head, hanging down in long locks, covered his back and shoulders, and the hair of his upper lip, being parted on both sides, lay upon his breast. His unbroken spirit, and noble demeanour, when addressing Claudius, commanded the admiration of that assembly that held in its hands the destinies of the world. But while such things are being enacted in the Roman Senate, another scene, only a few paces distant, we may here descry. In a dark vault cut out of the solid rock of the Capitoline Hill, there is a dungeon, called the Mamertine prison. In this dark cell many a vanquished prince had expiated with death the crime of being the enemy of Rome. Here at this time sat one who held in his hands a power that was destined to change the face of the world. Only a few yards of space and prison-walls are between the British captives and St. Paul, yet what an eternity of difference between them—the one representing the old order with its dreams and nightmares soon to pass away; the other the new order, fresh from Heaven, to arise in its place. As to Caradoc, his life is spared. He remains at Rome for some time, in the highest esteem, and vanishes henceforth from the page of history. Not so his family; for if a popular tradition condensed in the Welsh Triads is to be credited, Bran, his father, after seven years spent in Rome, returned, no longer a heathen, but a Christian, lighting up with his radiant presence the darkness that brooded over this realm. On the whole, we regard this personage as shadowy. He passes before us in so unsubstantial a form, with such a flitting touch, that he can scarcely be said to have established a right of way into the field of history. Two fair competitors, however, for the honour of introducing Christianity into Britain, next emerge before us, and appear on the dark background as angels of light, opening the eyes of our benighted countrymen to the light and the glory and the "sacred sweets" of the hill of Zion. Pomponia Græcina, the wife of Aulus Plautius, the first governor of Britain, and one of the most distinguished of Claudius' generals, and Claudia, the wife of Pudens, supposed to be the daughter of Caractacus, are credited with being the first heralds of the Gospel in Britain, at a time when St. Paul had many converts in Rome, and some even in "Cæsar's household." The former of these two noble ladies, whose fair hands sowed the precious seed in our Paganised soil, was soon brought to trial for having embraced the "foreign superstition," as Christianity was then termed by such writers as Suetonius and Pliny, and, though acquitted, it is sadly suggestive to read, in the pages of Tacitus, that "her life was protracted through a long course of melancholy years." We have already mentioned Claudia as the probable daughter of Caractacus, and the wife of Pudens. This Pudens was formerly called Rufus, but received the former name, it is said, on account of his modesty and gentleness. In the year 60, A.D., it is curious to note, St. Paul says, in his Epistle to the Romans, "Salute Rufus." But, six years afterwards, in the Second Epistle to Timothy, he says. "Eubulus greeteth thee, and Pudens, and Linus, and Claudia." Of Claudia, again, it is said by Martial, that master of epigram,

> " From painted Britons, how was Claudia born !
> The fair barbarian, how do arts adorn."

Then, in reference to her marriage :—

> " O Rufus ! Pudens whom I own my friend,
> Has ta'en the foreign Claudia for his wife.
> Propitious Hymen, light thy torch, and send
> Long years of bliss to their united life."

Thus the Roman power, like a huge storm-cloud darkening our sky, sent out its electric flashes through the gloom, and from that moment all things here were launched on a sea of change, in which much of our past was to be relegated to the lumber-room of creation, as a waste of unreality; while the Grand Reality began to dawn out of the darkness, and the germ of a slowly-developing kingdom of truth became rooted in the soil.

I now advert to that episode in the campaign which marks the expiring agonies of the Druid superstition, in which, closely pressed by the Roman power, it appears like a fugitive, which, in its wild terror, turns corner after corner to evade its pursuers, its whole appearance being that of a thing in the act of vanishing. The Druids were established in the Isle of Anglesea, whither the baffled forces of the Britons, chased before the victorious Romans, betook themselves for refuge. Suetonius, the Roman general under Nero, pushing on his conquests, resolved to reduce this stronghold to his sway. The Britons, nerved by despair, called to their aid both the force of arms and the terrors of superstition. In that last stronghold of the Druids a strange weird scene presents itself. The women and priests are intermingled with the soldiers upon the shore; and, running about with flaming torches in their hands and tossing their dishevelled hair, they struck greater terror into the astonished Romans by their howlings, cries, and execrations, than the real danger from the armed forces was able to inspire. But the event, as usual, was with the civilised discipline of Rome. The Britons are driven from their last refuge. The Druids are burned in the fires prepared by them for their enemies, and their sacred groves and consecrated altars are destroyed. While the fury of the Roman power was thus discharging itself in the west, the Britons were rallying their scattered forces in the east, where a British Deborah, Boadicea, smarting under cruel wrongs inflicted by the enemy, took the field. Under the inspiration of this Celtic heroine, several settlements of the conquerors were attacked with success, while London, already a flourishing Roman colony, was reduced to ashes, its inhabitants, the Romans, and all strangers, being put to the sword. This Suetonius speedily avenged in a great and decisive battle, where 80,000 of the Britons perished, and Boadicea herself, that "deceitful lioness," as the Saxon monk Gildas defames her, rather than fall into the hands of the enraged victor, put an end to her life by poison. Poor Boadicca! with no Claudia near, no angel form to cheer thee, no light to illumine thy dark soul. The old order was doomed. The sword that was to strike the blow was hanging from the smiling heavens. Beside the sacred lamp of Divine truth held in front of the gloom by two of the galaxy of Briton's daughters, thy sisters, thou art gone down to the realm of everlasting night; and yet, for thee, too, though a lost babe in the wood, there is a Father on high. We commit thee to Him, and take farewell of thee for ever, only casting one last glance behind on the page of history to see in thy lot a meteoric career, ending in disaster!

CHAPTER IV.

IT is matter of notoriety, as Fuller observes, that as the heathen, in searching after the original of their nations, never leave soaring "till they touch the clouds, and fetch their pedigree from some god, so Christians think it nothing worth except they relate the first planting to some Apostles." I have already suggested one point of contact between Christianity and Paganism in this land, in the persons of Pomponia Græcina and Claudia, two British Christians who were in Rome during the Apostle Paul's first imprisonment there. The credit, however, of first bringing the Gospel into Britain has been claimed for St. Peter, St. Philip, Simon Zelotes, Joseph of Arimathea, and especially St. Paul. On this point the same quaint writer quoted above, says :— "The British Church hath forgotten her own infancy, who were her first god-fathers. We see the light of the Word shined here, but we see not who kindled it."

The conversion of King Lucius, in the latter half of the second century, forms an important era in the history of the Celtic Church in Britain, especially if

Nennius is to be believed when he says that "all the chiefs of the British people received baptism with him." The testimony of Bede is that " Lucius, King of the Britons, sent a letter to Eleutherius, Bishop of Rome, 'entreating that, by his command, he might be made a Christian.'" "The reason," says Fuller, "why he wrote to Rome, was because at this time the church therein was (she can ask no more ; we grant no less) the most eminent church in the world, shining the brighter because set on the highest candlestick—the imperial city." Lucius, thus desirous to "put on the sweet yoke of our Saviour," and become a "nursing father" to the infant church in Briton, soon obtained the object of his pious request; and "the Britons," says Bede, "preserved the faith which they had received, uncorrupted and entire, in peace and tranquility, until the time of the Emperor Diocletian." In the "Welsh Triads" the foundation of the Church at Llandaff is attributed to him ; and though the traditionary accounts of the period must be received with great caution, it is interesting to note that under his reign "lands and civil privileges" were bestowed on the Christians, and that many Pagan temples were converted into Christian Churches, particularly that dedicated to Diana, now St. Paul's, London, and another consecrated to Apollo, now Westminster Abbey. Though, as we have already indicated, the traditional accounts are "full of dross," yet they are not summarily to be dismissed, as if they were altogether dreams. "We dare not," says Fuller, "wholly deny the substance of the story, though the leaven of monkery hath much swollen and puffed up the circumstance thereof."

There is reason to believe that since Christianity first dwelt here it has never departed hence, that, like the "candle of the virtuous wife" mentioned in the Book of Proverbs, "It went not out by night." Though as to the *personnel* of those who were instrumental in first lighting up our land we know little or nothing, the merest "glimmer of light" being fitfully thrown on a few individuals and localities. Though these, in the traditional accounts, are like "finger-posts dim seen," on a moorland journey, "through gathering fogs," yet as we have seen the lighting of the streets of a town, how when the first lamp is lit it is plainly seen dispelling the surrounding darkness; but when the second, third, fourth, and all the lamps are lit, light meets light, ray blends with ray, until the whole place is illuminated, so was it with the spread of Christian light in this country in the second and third centuries. At Glastonbury, Llandaff, St. Albans, York, and London, the lamp of Divine Truth was early lighted; and from these centres of illumination the gloom was pierced, and began to yield to the power of Him who first said to the chaos and darkness of the new-born world, "Let there be light." A rapid glance at the progress made by Christianity in this country up to its establishment by Constantine will conclude this chapter.

Ireneus, bishop of Lyons, who was but one step

removed from St. John, having been a disciple of
Polycarp, who was himself taught by that Apostle,
bears testimony to the spread of Christianity in
Britain in his day; while Tertullian, of Carthage, the
embodiment of the highest learning of his age, speaks
of the Christian Church in the second century as having extended to "all the boundaries of Spain, and the
different nations of Gaul, and *parts of Britain inaccessible to the Romans*, but subject to Christ." Origen,
too, whom Jerome styles "a man of immortal genius,"
thus speaks of Christianity in Britain in his time
(third century):—"The power of our Lord and
Saviour is with those who in Britain are separated
from our coasts."

Though, as already hinted, we know very little of
those who were instrumental in founding and extending the Christian system in this country, whoever
they were, they must have been possessed of a measure
of faith and courage, entitling them to the rank of
heroes. They advanced to the work, as already observed, between the two fires of Roman and Druid
opposition. Gildas, in speaking of the severities of
the Pagan persecution at the beginning of the fourth
century under Diocletian, says:—"The whole Church
seemed to be under execution, and, charging bravely
through this ill-natured and inhospitable world,
marched, as it were, in whole bodies to heaven." As
for the British Christians, he says—"Many were
despatched with diversity of torture, and torn limb
from limb in a most barbarous and cruel manner;

that those who escaped the fury of their persecutors retired to woods and deserts, and hid themselves in caves, where they continued confessors till God was pleased 'to bring better times to the Church.'"

St. Albans, in Hertfordshire, is the birth-place of Britain's proto-martyr. His story is touching. While still a Pagan he gave shelter to a Christian minister, whom he found in a state of destitution, pursued by the fierce idolaters, on account of his religion. In this way Alban came under the influence of the Gospel, and he became a Christian. And when the guest whom he sheltered was traced, and the Roman soldiers appeared on the scene to apprehend him, Alban arrayed himself in the robes of his Christian teacher, and was seized by the officers and carried before the governor. On being asked his name, he said—"My name is Alban, and I worship the only true and living God, who created all things." And when the Magistrate urged him to sacrifice to the gods of Rome, he answered—"The sacrifices you offer are made to devils; neither can they help the needy, or grant the petitions of their votaries. I am a Christian." On this the governor was so enraged, that he ordered him immediately to be beheaded. The place where he suffered was on a hill overlooking the spot then occupied by the ancient Verulam.

> "Thus was Alban tried,
> England's first martyr, whom no threats could shake ;
> Self-offered victim, for his friend he died,
> And for the faith—nor shall his name forsake
> That hill—whose flowery platform seems to rise
> By nature decked for holiest sacrifice."

Thus beautiful is Wordsworth's tribute to one of Britain's noblest sons—her first martyr.

After the death of Diocletian the Church had a breathing time from persecution. The father of Constantine, according to the testimony of Eusebius, "preserved such religious people as were under his command without any hurt or harm." And this happy state of things was made universal when Constantine, born in Britain, and of a British mother, attained to the Imperial throne. He "first turned the tide in the whole world, and not only quenched the fire, but even overturned the furnace of persecution, and enfranchised Christianity throughout the Roman empire." Then it was that "the faithful Christians, who, during the time of danger, had hidden themselves in woods, deserts, and secret caves, appearing in public, rebuilt the churches that had been levelled to the ground; and all the Church's sons rejoiced, as it were, in the fostering bosom of a mother." And whereas none were found to softly rock the infant Church, or sing sweet lullabies by its cradle, now it comes forth in majesty, the joy of all the land, and is lifted to honour in the Roman State ; so that, as it has been quaintly said, "The Gospel, formerly a forester, now became a citizen ; and, leaving the woods wherein it wandered, hills and holes where it hid itself before, dwelt quietly in populous places." The panegyrist of Constantine, Eumenius Rhetor, thus speaks in an oration addressed to that emperor,—" O fortunata et nunc omnibus beatior terris Britanniæ

Constantinum Cæsarem vidisti"—"O, happy Britain,
and blessed above all other lands, which didst first
behold Constantine Cæsar." Without committing ourselves to any extravagant laudation of this, the first
Christian emperor that ruled over the empire, it may
suffice here to be remembered that one of his first
acts, when he succeeded to the Imperial throne, was
to put an end to the persecution of the Christians;
and that one of the earliest efforts put forth by the
Church, then first established by him, was to purge
itself from Arianism.

CHAPTER V.

IN my last sketch I endeavoured to trace the foundations of the Celtic Church in Britain. In order to do this I gave a rapid survey of the dawn and early development of Christianity in Britain up to the date of its establishment under Constantine. I now propose to call a halt in the historical narrative, and from the standpoint of philosophy, to bestow a passing glance at the general situation—to penetrate beneath the veil of historic fact, and stand for a little in front of ultimate principles; to lay bare before the mind's eye those forces that were in operation in the rise and development of the aboriginal superstition; to trace the influences of the Pagan mythology in modifying that system of nature worship; to map out the various theological and philosophical currents whose united stream determined the course of Christian thought in early times. Only thus can we hope to arrive at an intelligible conception of Christianity in its relation to human thought, and see the picture with its appropriate background, the organism and its environment. In this way also shall we detect the presence and influence of those infecting elements which, from the malaria of human speculation, early diffused their poison in the system of Divine truth, and sent Christianity to bed under various forms of disease called heresies. As we look back on that far distant "distracted cloudy imbroglio" of Paganism in which our ancestors were enveloped, it seems more like a cloudland than a continent of firm land and facts. Yet in that far-off "confused rumour of Pagan ages," we shall hear, if we turn to it with affectionate earnestness, some feeble echo of truth; something leading us up to the belief that there was a kind of fact at the heart of it. To the first Pagan thinker, simple, open as a child, yet with the depth and strength of a man, nature in all its departments was a great mystery. It had as yet no name. The infinite variety of sights, sounds, shapes, and motions, which we now collectively call the Universe, was not as yet veiled under any formula. "It stood naked, flashing in on him there, beautiful, awful, unspeakable." "Canopus," says Carlyle, "shining down over the desert, with its blue diamond brightness, would pierce into the heart of the wild Ishmaelitish man whom it was guiding through the solitary waste there. To his wild heart, with all feelings in it, with no speech for any feeling, it might seem a little eye, that Canopus, glancing out on him from the great deep Eternity; revealing the inner splendour to him. Cannot we understand how these men *worshipped* Canopus; became what we call Sabeans, worshipping the stars? Such is to me the secret of all forms of Paganism. Worship is transcendent wonder. . . To these primæval men, all things, and everything they saw exist beside them, were an emblem of the Godlike, of some God. The science of their thoughts on religion consisted in a recognition of the forces of nature as Godlike, stupendous, personal agencies—as gods and demons. Carrying such thoughts and feelings with them when they left their original home in the east, time and circumstances moulded them into new forms and features, they entered into new combinations, they were modified by interaction with special varieties of the original forms. Their attitude to nature remained the same; but, in a downward movement, their thoughts gravitated towards its weird-like aspects. The mountain storm, the thunder-cloud, the dark hostile powers of nature established a grim tyranny over the minds of the ancient Britons. Out of the dark interior of their thoughts spectral forms crept forth; and with these they populated nature. That region of a man's nature which has to do with the unknown was in their case lighted up with lurid smoke-flame, a scene of terror reflecting nature as an army of hostile powers, watching for man's ruin. In the dark forests whence at nightfall crept forth the wolf and the fox; in every "cranny and doghole" of nature, demons were ready to spring forth for the destruction of man. Of the quaint memorials of this devil worship in which our barbarian ancestors were enslaved, we have an account by Gildas, who says that the pictures of those

C

devils worshipped by the Britons remained in his day within and without the decayed walls of their cities, "drawn with deformed faces (no doubt done to the life according to their terrible apparitions), so that such ugly shapes did not woo, but frighten people into adoration of them." But the Romans brought their own gods with them when they invaded this land, and the rude old myths of a degenerate Druidism were not strong enough to stand against the classical mythology. Sprung from the same old root, this form of religion, under the influence of an incipient hero-worship, the "grand modifying element in that ancient system of thought," has given birth to Jupiter the great father whose realm is the upper sky; Apollo, identified with the sun; Juno, who pervades the nether atmosphere, and so forth. In the Oriental system nature stands as the emblem of God; religion is the poetical interpretation of the universe. In the Roman system, which assimilated that of the Greeks, there is the conception of man as a predominant element. If nature be a symbol of God, man is a higher emblem still. What the "golden-mouthed" St. Chrysostome said in reference to the Shekinah or ark of testimony, the visible revelation of God among the Hebrews, contains a deeply significant and eternal truth. He says, "The true Shekinah is man!" "And truly this is no vain phrase," says Carlyle, "it is even so. The essence of our being, the mystery in us that calls itself 'I'—ah, what words have we for such things?—is a breath of Heaven; the Highest Being

reveals himself in man, . . . is not that the germ of
Christianity itself ? The greatest of all heroes is one
—whom we do not name here! Let sacred silence,"
he characteristically adds, "meditate that sacred matter." When we go far enough back in our historical
investigations, we at length reach a region in which
fact and fable are so blended, a kind of debateable
land on which the mists and fogs of time so rest, that
it is impossible to separate the one from the other,
the fact from the fable, the nucleus of truth from the
accretions of error. This land is peopled by what are
called in the classical literature of antiquity heroes,
concerning whom it may often be matter of doubt
whether they are gods come down to men, or men
who have, by the popular imagination, been elevated
into gods. And this interaction of Eastern and Western thought that entered into the early formation of
Greek mythology and Roman Paganism, may have
taken up and assimilated in its growth the pervading
element of Judaism—the Messianic idea—which, by
tradition, finding its way to the Greek mind, accen-
tuated, and fixed more clearly the lines in which the
development of the heroic mythology proceeded. The
parent stream of Oriental thought, with its nature
worship, had thus far its tributary streams; first, the
conception of man as the emblem of God, from the
west (Greeks and Romans), then the Messianic idea,
the essential feature of which is " Emanuel, God
with us," from the Hebrews. Through various
changes and modifications had the old mythology

passed when Britain was in the fast grip of the
Roman power; but these three elements, in their interaction and combination, formed the great dynamic
force in the religious life of our ancestors when Christianity was introduced into our island. Its historical
aspect, its outward expression and embodiment, belongs to a region of conjecture—a region where we
have not even probability as a guide—a morass of
uncertainty, where all footing yields; but when we
contemplate it from the standpoint of philosophy, we
seem to get a glimpse of the soul or fact which con-
stituted its essential characteristic, and which, though
merged in the world's broad stream of thought, was
not without its own local colouring. When the pure
rays of Christian light fell on this mingled stream of
paganised thought, they were refracted as light is
when transmitted through media of varying density,
and the heresies that emerged tell the story in an
objective way of the interaction of religious thought
which a subjective forecast of the situation would
seem to have pointed out as the natural resultant of
the forces in operation. Seen in this light, the Arian
and Pelagian heresies, which early appeared in this
country, will seem as the natural growth of what was
already in the soil. Oriental theosophy, Greek philosophy, especially that of Plato, and the Jewish Cabala,
were blended in a general system of thought, which,
emanating from the schools of Alexandria, extended
in all directions, touching Christian thought at different points, and mingling with the Christian doc-

trines in varying proportions. This system was called Gnosticism, and embraced various shades of religious thought according to the various proportions in which the distinctively Christian elements entered into the combination with those which were purely Pagan. Thus among the early Gnostics there were those who were almost altogether Pagan, others who were almost altogether Christian, with every intermediate shade between the two.

The heresies that emerged in the early development of Christianity had reference generally to the founder of the Christian system, the doctrines of the Divine grace, and the providence of God. They included schools of thought, known as Socinianism, Sabellianism, Arianism, Pelagianism, and Manicheism, etc, etc. The first three systems in the above enumeration, and which were the offspring of Gnosticism, had reference to the person of our Lord and the doctrine of the Trinity. Pelagianism, which reflected the Greek idea of self-development, was in sharp contrast with the Calvinistic view of grace, otherwise called the Evangelical School of Christian thought; while Manicheism, imported from Persia, consisted in a combination of the dual conception of the system of Zoroaster with that of the Divine unity and sovereignty as embodied in Christianity. At the back of Phenomena, and the origin of things, Manes, or Manicheus, saw the good God and the bad devil. He agreed with the orthodox in referring the good in the world to God the bad to the devil; but whereas in the orthodox Christian system the devil is subordinate to God, in the system of Manicheus, both powers hold co-ordinate jurisdiction. This system is the result of human thought in its attitude to the universe as presenting a struggle detween light and darkness, and good and evil; it is the solution arrived at by one section of the human race of that dark problem which has engaged the minds of men in all ages, the existence and origin of evil. It is that form of the solar myth that has found expression in the system of the Magi; and it is just possible that the sunrise and sunset, the daily return of day and night, the battle between light and darkness, the whole solar drama in all its details, that is acted every day, every month, every year, in heaven and in earth, was one great germinal principle in that ancient aboriginal superstition of Britain, in which, as we have seen, devil worship and magic were conspicuous elements. Though this system of Manicheus does not seem, in early Christian times, to have established for itself in Britain a "local habitation and a name," its spirit has tinged the thoughts of all men in all ages, from the time that Job and his friends looked out upon the universe, and were perplexed by the appearances of suffering and moral evil that met their gaze, until now, when men see in development and evolution streaks of light breaking through the darkness of this problem. It has permeated the atmosphere both of belief and unbelief in all ages. If John Stuart Mill discovered spots in the sun, points at which Divine power fails, goodness retires from the field, and the Deity is forced to struggle, we get a glimpse in this way of the relation in which the system of Manes stands to the universe. And when the artist talks of nature, the philosopher of law, and unskilled theologians of the devil, we have an example, in different departments, of a survival of the ancient Persian mode of thought, in which we have a dual government of the world, and in which God tends to become more and more a remote and misty phantom.

A few words regarding the other heresies in the above enumeration will conclude this sketch. As to the person of the Founder of Christianity, four theories may be held. He may be regarded as really human, but not divine; 2, really divine, but not human; 3, neither human nor divine; or 4, both human and divine. These, the only possible theories on the subject, have, strange to say, all actually been maintained in the Church in the process of its development. The first of these views, that which affirms the human nature of Jesus, but denies His divinity, was held by a small sect of Jewish converts called the Ebionites, who flourished in the first century. According to the testimony of Eusebius, Theodotus was the first who taught the simple humanity of Christ — the doctrine of modern Unitarians. The second view, according to which the divinity of Christ is asserted, and His humanity denied, was held in the second century by Praxeas, and in the third century by Noetus and Sabellius. The term Sabellianism in-

cludes this view in a larger conception in which the
Trinity is regarded as not consisting of three persons,
but of one person in three aspects. Swedenborgianism
is the modern representative of this view. Between
these two extremes religious thought oscillated, and
before the Nicene Council, gravitated, in great volume,
towards that system which, from the name of its
founder, is called Arianism. According to this view
Jesus is not human, nor divine, but a being, *sui
generis*, intermediate between God and man, the most
exalted of the creatures, but still only a creature.
This view, which represents the Christian consciousness in a nebulous condition, before the system of
Christian doctrine emerged in clear and distinct form,
was condemned, as already stated, by the Council of
Nicea A.D. 325, and the orthodox view affirmed.
Hitherto the Church in Britain continued sound and
orthodox, and was in no degree tainted with heresy.
But towards the latter half of the fourth century, "the
gangrene of the Arian heresy began to spread itself
into this island." "Naturalists," says Fuller, "dispute
how wolves had their first being in Britain, it being
improbable that merchants would bring any such
noxious vermin over in their ships, and impossible
that of themselves they should swim over the sea, . .
. . . but here the query may be propounded, how
these heretics (mystical 'wolves not sparing the
flocks,' Acts 20-29) first entered into this island.
And indeed, we meet neither with their names nor
manner of transportation hither, but only with the

cursed fruits of their labours." Then follows an ob-
servation of our author, conceived in the true spirit
of the friends of Job, that "immediately after this
kingdom was infected with Arianism, the Pagan Picts
and Scots out of the north made a general and despe-
rate invasion of it; it being just with God, when His
vineyard beginneth to bring forth wild grapes, then
to let loose the wild boar, to take his full and free
repast upon it." While the Arian heresy was thus an
importation, Pelagianism—so called from Pelagius, the
classical form in which the name of its founder has
been handed down—was a native of the soil. The
author of this system was said to be a monk of
Bangor, called Morgan, which, in Welsh, signifies "near
the sea;" "and well had it been for the Christian
world," says the same quaint writer already quoted,
"if he had been nearer the sea, and served therein as
the Egyptians served the Hebrew males." This heresy
represents the interaction of Greek thought with revealed truth. In it Greek thought is free from the
Oriental element except in regard to its ascetic tendency. The ethics of self-development is the essential
characteristic of the system of Pelagius. In it the
gospel of self-help neutralised the doctrines of the
Divine grace. The consequences of Adam's fall did not
overlap his own nature. No taint was thus communicated to the moral powers of man. Infants come into
the world occupying the same position as Adam did
before the fall; they are baptised, not to be freed
from sin, but thereby to be adopted into the Kingdom

of God. Adam died, not by reason of sin, but by the condition of nature. In this system the doctrine of depravity is reduced to a minimum, and conversion is transformed into development. The disease of sin and its remedy alike recede into the background. A memorable circumstance related in this connection is that the "same day whereon Palagius was born in Britain, St. Augustine, his great antagonist, was also born in Africa; Divine Providence so disposing it that the poison and the antidote should be twins in a manner, in respect of the same time." While this heresy has never been held by any distinct and separate community of professing Christians in the sense of being the Shibboleth of a sect, it has been a fruitful source of controversy in all ages of the Church, entering, as it has done, as an element into many various and even diverse schools of Christian thought, so that, according to Fuller, simply to recount the learned works which have been written on this subject "would amount to a volume fitter for a porter's back to bear than a scholar's brains to peruse."

CHAPTER VI.

THE present sketch will include a period of up-
wards of two centuries, dating from the Council
of Nicea, A.D. 325, to the arrival of St. Columba
at Iona, about the year A.D. 563. On the background
of our political history this interval is filled up with
striking transformations, in which we see the great
bell of time ringing out the Romans, and ringing in
the Saxons, and so producing a complete metamor-
phosis in the land. The Picts and Scots, the scourge
and terror of the Britons of the South, we see brought
under the benign influences of Christianity. St. Patrick in Ireland; St. Ninian and St. Columba and St.
Kentigern or Mungo in Scotland, light up with streaks
of golden brightness the "age and body" of their
times; dispelling the surrounding darkness, and sending a trail of light down through the ages. We see
the regret with which the Britons part with their
masters the Romans, and the fierce struggle with
which, for more than a century, the land was con-
vulsed by her Saxon invaders. In connection with
the main road along which the history of the Church

proceeds, there are many romantic byepaths which lie invitingly open, which, however, must not be suffered to tempt us to stray beyond the smallest limits in tracts that are purely secular. The exploits of Arthur —the twelve pitched battles in which he defeated the Pagan Saxons, with all the halo of romance that surrounds the "Knights of the Round Table," we must not bestow a thought upon, except to say of the Monks who have so over-embellished this subject, that "the very truths which they have written of him are discredited, because found in company with so many lies." During this period the history of the Church in Britain is involved in some obscurity. In the space of 200 years, there is but little of solid history. A few *quasi* facts lost in a wilderness of padding is the aspect of things presented to us in the dust heap whence our materials are unearthed. "But," as Fuller quaintly says, "as I find little, so I will feign nothing, time being better spent in silence than in lying." What we can discern very clearly is, that during this time the Church was outwardly afflicted by Picts, Scots, and Saxons, and inwardly harassed by the Arian and Pelagian heresies. The decisive defeat sustained by Galgacus at the foot of the Grampians in the year 84 A.D. placed Britain in the fast grip of the Roman power. Julius Agricola, by whom this was accomplished, knowing the fierce and indomitable character of the Picts and Scots in the North, fixed a chain of garrisons between the Firths of Clyde and Forth, the better to secure the Roman Province of the

south from the incursions of these wild barbarians.
A wall was afterwards erected along the line of the
forts by Antoninus Pius, which, with one previously
built by Adrian, between the Tyne and the Solway,
enclosed the Roman province of Valentia. Thus the
rights of savage freedom were contracted to the
narrow limits of Caledonia; at least, so the Romans
imagined. These rude ancestors of ours, however
"stern and wild" as their native land, refused to be
crammed up in the north in that way, and like a
wild beast ever ready to burst its chains, were a perpetual menace to their southern neighbours. The
Dutch dykes have been found capable of keeping out
the sea, but the wild impetuosity of these savage Caledonians could not be checked by a "scientific frontier."
Ever and anon they burst forth from their fastnesses
in the north, spreading terror and dismay everywhere
from the wall of Antoninus to the shores of Kent.
During the Roman occupation, indeed, these incursions were checked as the tide is by the cliffs on the
beach, but on the withdrawal of that power the South
Britons were helpless to resist their encroachments,
which were as surging waves beating on a flat and
defenceless shore. For though the Romans left the
country well provided for its defence, they were without the spirit or power of resistance; so that when
the keels of the Roman vessels quitted the British
strand, and both nations felt that the parting was
final, the cliffs and shores of Britain were as thickly
crowded by mourners for the departure of the Romans,

as they had been nearly five centuries before by despe-
rate opponents of their first landing. When we lift
the veil at this point, and take a glance at the situation of affairs in South Britain after the retirement of
the Romans, we see under a "dim," but by no means
a "religious light," various independent and rival
communities formed—nearly 200 kinglings sometimes
united in their jealousies of some paramount tyrant,
but more frequently raging among themselves. Thus
we find "The Lioness of Devonshire" encountering a
"Lion's whelp," and the "Bear-Baiter" humbling before his regal brother "The great Bull Dog!" This
is the scene that presents itself to us when they were
let alone by their neighbours; but a darker aspect is
observed when we contemplate them after the preda-
tory exploits of the Picts and Scots, when famine and
death, the attendants of war, were so rife that there
were "scarcely living enough to bury the dead." In
their extremity British ambassadors are despatched to
Rome "in a mournful manner, with their garments
rent, and sand on their heads," humbly imploring that
they would not permit so ancient a province to become
a prey and a scorn to barbarians. Their prayer was
heard. The Romans came to their assistance now for
the second time since their departure; but told them
plainly that in the future they must help themselves,
as no more aid from Rome need be expected. The
truth was that the old empire was in the throes of
dissolution. "The new Babylon, rival of the old,
swelled out like her with her successes, and triumph-

ing in her pleasures and riches, was about to encounter as great a fall." Alaric the Goth, Attila the Hun, Genseric the Vandal, found it like a huge weight on the top of an inclined plane, ready to go down with the slightest push. Nobody could hold out a hand to avert the judgment that was about to fall on that great power, the mistress and tyrant of the world. "The plain truth," says Fuller, "is that the Roman Empire, now grown ruinous, could not repair its out-rooms, and was fain to let them fall down, to maintain the rest; and, like the fencers receiving a blow on their leg to save their head, exposed the remote countries of Spain, France, and Britain, to the spoil of Pagans, to secure the seat of Empire." Another piti-ful appeal is made to Rome on a fresh invasion of the Picts and Scots, but this time in vain. The appeal was clamant, but the Romans had more than enough to do at home. The appeal, addressed to the Consul Ætius, thus proceeds:—"To Ætius, thrice consul, the Groanes of the Brittaines." "The Barbarians drive us back to the sea—the sea again putteth us back upon the Barbarians; thus, between two kinds of death, we are either slaughtered or drowned, etc." After the failure of this melancholy appeal, the Britons were reduced to the utmost despair, by intelligence that the Scots, who had always retired within their own northern confines, after pillaging and destroying at their pleasure, were now assembling a large army for the purpose of extirpating the natives, and settling great numbers of their own people in Britain. What

was to be done ? Their leaders were assembled together in serious consultation as to how the impending
ruin was to be averted. Roman aid failed them ; self-
help found no place in their counsels, when at length
Vortigern, a British king, a man of considerable influence among his countrymen, doomed himself to a fatal
celebrity by being the first to suggest the "destructive
project," which brought the "Dragons of Germany"
(as the bards called the Saxons) as friends and allies
into Britain. Over they came in response to the
invitation of the Britons, first in three great ships
under Hengist and Horsa, their leaders. The island
of Thanet in Kent, their landing-place, became their
first possession ; "but," says Fuller, "following afterwards in such swarms that quickly they grew formid-
able to him that invited them over, of guests turning
sojourners, then inmates, and lastly landlords, till they
had dispossessed the Britons of the best part of the
island."

With the fall of the empire we see a new departure
in the evolution of events in the rise of modern states ;
and as the shores of Wigtown Bay form an inlet to the
Atlantic, so the Saxon invasion of Britain was a con-
tribution from the main stream of progress, of which
the Saxon Heptarchy was the symbol and expression.
While such commotions agitated the State, the decline of the Church was perhaps inevitable. For, as
Fuller quaintly observes, " He who expects a flourishing Church in a failing commonwealth, let him try
whether one side of his face can smile, when the

other is pinched." The fact is, the life of the Church
is a drama in which great inward modifications ac-
company outward changes. The sanguinary devasta-
tion, first by the Picts and Scots, and afterwards by
the Saxons, in the first half of the fifth century, reduced the British Church to the greatest straits. The
aim of the Saxons, whose help had been invoked to
beat back the Picts and Scots, was nothing else than
the subjugation of the ancient inhabitants of Britain
under their dominion. For 130 years, during which
the war lasted, the Church continued to shrink before
the intruders within the remote fastnesses of Wales
and Cornwall. Britain became involved, from east to
west, in rapine and slaughter; her cruel masters turned
their ruthless hands against every person and thing
that had a religious character, destroyed every Church
they could reach, and slew the Christians at the very
altar; the ministers were hunted down like wild beasts,
and either perished miserably or sought refuge in ex-
patriation. With the race of the ancient inhabitants
disappeared the refinements of society introduced by
the Romans. To the worship of the true God succeeded the impure rites of Woden; and the barbarism
and ignorance of the north of Germany were trans-
planted into the most flourishing provinces of Britain.
Yet, in the overshadowing darkness, quite a brilliant
galaxy of luminaries appear, among whom we descry
Dubricius, with his academy in Monmouthshire, a seat
of piety and learning, where many disciples were
taught the elements of human and divine learning.

St. David, uncle to King Arthur, and, like his nephew,
lost in a dreamland of legend; St. Petrock of Cornwall, the "cornucopia of saints," whose parishes carry
sanctity in their names; St. Kentigern, otherwise
called St. Mungo, the famous Bishop of Ellwye in
North Wales, and patron saint of Glasgow, besides
many other men, may be mentioned as handling down
the sacred tradition, even in those times of darkness
and tumult. "But," as Fuller observes, "a national
church, being a large room, it is hard to count all the
candles God lighted therein."

We have seen that the troubles of the State were
such as to necessitate the aid of strangers. The
Britons were unable to cope with the Picts and Scots
by themselves, but sought aid first from the Romans,
and, when that power failed them, from the Saxons.
Strange to say, a similar impotence unnerved the
Church when subjected to the troubles of heresy.
The scholarship of its ministers seems to have halted
a little behind the wonders of antiquity. The Arian
heresy, as was before noted, was proscribed at the
Council of Nicea, A.D. 325. It was between the years
420 and 430 that the British Church was infected
with Pelagianism; and the orthodox clergy, being
unable to stem its progress, sent to Gaul, desiring
assistance. In a full synod of the Gallican Church, it
was determined that Germanus, bishop of Auxerre,
and Lupus, bishop of Troyes, should be sent to Britain
to confute the heretics. These holy men were pre-
vented for some time from approaching the shores of

Britain by a dreadful tempest, but at length they made their destined port in fair weather, when they found the beach crowded with friends ready to welcome them. A meeting was immediately appointed by the British clergy for public disputation with the Pelagians at *Verulam*, now St. Albans. The Pelagians, according to the testimony of Bede, came to the council in great pomp, and advocated their cause with most inflated rhetoric; but Germanus and Lupus, when it was their turn to reply, so overwhelmed them with arguments and authorities that they were completely silenced, and the whole assembly triumphed in their discomfiture. About this time the Pagan Picts, with some straggling Saxons (who had come over to pillage on their own account before they were united under Hengist and Horsa), having attacked the Britons, the latter implored the assistance of Germanus and Lupus, who immediately complied with their request, and repaired to their camp. In these days of "Salvation Armies" it may be interesting to relate an episode which is unique in Church history, and which is entitled the "Alleluiatic victory." The narrative is that of Constantius of Lyons, the biographer of St. Germanus, and who wrote while several persons were alive who had been acquainted with that prelate. "The sacred days of Lent were at hand, which the presence of the divines, Germanus and Lupus, rendered more solemn, insomuch that those instructed by their daily preaching, flocked eagerly to the grace of baptism, for the great multitude of the army was desirous of the water of the laver of salvation. A church formed of interwoven branches of trees is prepared against the day of the resurrection of our Lord, and though the expedition was encamped in the field, is fitted up like that of a city. The army, wet with baptism, advances. The people are fervent in faith, and, neglecting the protection of arms, they await the assistance of the Deity. In the meantime this plan of proceeding, or state of the camp, is reported to the enemy, who, anticipating a victory over an unarmed multitude, hasten with alacrity. But their approach is discovered by the scouts, and when, after concluding the solemnities of Easter, the greater part of the army, fresh from their baptism, were preparing to take up arms and give battle, Germanus offers himself as the leader of the war." Then follows an exaggerated description of the route of the enemy, upon whose approach Germanus assembled the British troops in a hollow dale in Flintshire, surrounded with hills, with instructions that, at a signal given, they should all shout *Hallelujah* three times, which was faithfully obeyed. The Pagans were surprised with the suddenness and loudness of the sound, which was much multiplied by the advantage of the echo, whereby their fear brought in a false list of their enemies' number; and, rather trusting their ears than their eyes, they reckoned their foes by the increase of the noise rebounded unto them; and then, allowing two hands for every mouth, how vast was their army! But, besides the *concavity* of the valley improving the

sound, " God sent a hollowness," says Fuller, " into the
hearts of the Pagans; so that their apprehensions
added to their ears, and cowardice often resounded
the same shout in their breasts, till, beaten with the
reverberation thereof, without striking a stroke, they
confusedly ran away; and many were drowned for
speed in the river Alen, lately the Christians' font,
now the Pagans' grave.   Thus a bloodless victory was
gotten, without sword drawn, consisting of no fight,
but a _fright_, and a _flight_; and that Hallelujah, the
song of the saints after conquest achieved (Rev. xix.
1) was here the forerunner and procurer of victory;
so good a _grace_ it is, to be said both before and after
a battle."   In these commotions the Celtic Church
was chased before the Saxon invaders, out of South
Britain.   " Religion now-a-days," says Fuller, " played
least in sight, hiding itself in holes; and the face of
the Church was so blubbered with tears, that she may
seem almost to have wept her eyes out, having lost
her seers and principal pastors; " but in Ireland, under
the labours of St. Patrick, as we shall presently see,
it flourished and extended itself in all directions.

A very dim figure is trotted out of obscurity, and
made to flit across the page of history at this point.
In the Anglo-Saxon Chronicle, we read: " A.D. 430.
This year, Palladius the Bishop was sent to the Scots
by Pope Celestinus, that he might confirm their faith."
He is also mentioned by Bede, Nennius, and others.
A difficulty arises here as to his destination, whether
it was Ireland, the land of the Scots, or the coast of

Argyll, where was a small colony of Scots,—probably both. According to Nennius, he seems to have encountered stormy weather when he tried to effect a a landing in Ireland; or, having settled there, not to have attained any great measure of success, and to have sought and found a new sphere of labour among the Picts. Tradition traces him to Fordoun, in the Mearns, where he was buried. The remains of a chapel dedicated to him are still pointed out in the churchyard of that parish. It, too, was the resort of pilgrims in mediæval times, from all parts of the country.

But a more substantial figure now emerges before our eyes, the famous St. Patrick, the Apostle of Ireland. Born most probably at Kilpatrick, on the Clyde, when he was sixteen years of age he was taken captive by some Irish pirates, and brought to Ireland. After six years he effected his escape and returned to his own country. But what he had seen in Ireland filled him with an intense desire to be employed as a Christian missionary there. To prepare himself for this purpose he passed into France, and spent some time under the tuition of his uncle, St. Martin of Tours. His original name is said to have been Succath, Patricius being the Roman appellative by which he was known. His name, Succath, is perpetuated in the district as the title of a property there. In the year 431 he went to Rome, whence he was sent by the Pope of the day, Celestine, to preach in Ireland, in which he succeeded Paladius. In his time a mighty change came over the face of Ireland. Religion flourished and spread into all parts. The threescore lives and ten which are said to have been written of this eminent saint doubtless contain much that sober piety cannot receive as authentic history. According to the accounts of his biographers, he went up and down the whole of Ireland, preaching the Gospel and founding churches. After 20 years labour, during which he founded 365 churches, and baptised with his own hands 12,000 persons, besides ordaining many priests, he fixed his seat at Armagh, about A.D. 454, and died at a place called Saul, near Downpatrick, where his relics were preserved down to the period of the Reformation. The only authentic literary remains of this saint that are now extant consist of his "Confession" and a letter addressed to Coroticus, who is supposed to have been a Welsh chieftain, who had made a descent on the Irish coast, and had slain or carried off amidst circumstances of great cruelty, a number of the Irish, many of whom were under his instruction.

Having thus traced the foundations of the early British or Celtic Church, we now follow the stream of events in connection with its rise and development in the northern part of our "Isle." St. Ninian, St. Mungo, and St. Columba are leaders in the noble army of those who, in the name of a higher power than that of Rome, invaded the shores of our barbarian ancestors and put them to the sword—the sword of the Spirit—and triumphed over them by Christianity and the Word of God.

According to Bede, the Southern Picts were converted by the preaching of St. Ninian, who was consecrated Bishop of Whithorn, in Galloway. Usher supposes that the sphere of his evangelistic labours extended from the modern Glasgow to Stanemore Cross, on the borders of Westmoreland. It seems to have exceeded these limits. Bede states that this "most reverend bishop and holy man of the British nation had been regularly instructed at Rome in the faith and mysteries of the truth ; that his Episcopal see was named after St. Martin the Bishop; that it was famous for a stately Church in which he and many other saints rest in the body; and that it was still in existence in his time." "The place," he further says, "belongs to the province of the Bernicians, and is generally called the White House, because he there built a church of stone, which was not usual among the Britons."

The time and place of his birth are doubtful, though, from his connection with St. Martin of Tours, who died about A.D. 400, we know that he must have flourished towards the close of the fourth century. His biography, written by Abbot Ailred, in the twelfth century, is not to be relied on as containing a faithful portraiture of his life. The floating traditions in which his memory was preserved during the ages which intervened between him and his biographer seem to have grown chiefly on the side of the marvellous. A few facts are given, served up with the usual sauce of the miraculous,—the omnipresent

element in the lives of the saints. He is said to have
visited Rome in his youth, where also he received his
early education. The Pope, learning that in some
parts of Britain there were people who had not yet
received the faith, and others who had only heard
the Gospel from heretics, armed him with a commis-
sion to convert his native country. On his way home
he visited the celebrated Martin of Tours, who was
then one of the leading men in the Church of Gaul.
By Martin, to whom he was related, he was instructed
in monastic discipline; and to him, perhaps, he owed
some of the enthusiasm he manifested in the great
work to which he had been consecrated. His return
home was hailed with great joy among all to whom
his wonderful devotion and saintly character were
known. Having established his residence in Galloway,
this holy man began in earnest the evangelistic
labours which, extending from the shores of the Solway to the southern slopes of the Grampians, resulted
in the conversion of the Southern Picts, thus furnish-
ing an additional instance of the truth of Tertullian's triumphant assertion two centuries before, that
"Chrstianity reigned in regions inaccessible to the
Roman arms."

Assisted by masons he brought with him from
France, he built the Church already mentioned as
the first stone edifice of the kind erected in the
country. From its white and glistening aspect, seen
over the Bay of Wigtown, it was called in Latin,
Candida Casa.

Such, then, are the meagre details history has pre-served regarding him who may be called the Great Pioneer of the Gospel to this land. The traditional aspects of his life I have already referred to in my introductory lecture. These are chiefly valuable as a testimony to the mark he made in his day and generation; a mark the memory of which has come down the ages, and made his shrine the attraction of pilgrims; and all who have felt the strain of clinging affection for the scene of a country's earliest contact with Christianity will be drawn to Whithorn as to holy ground.

A few years after St. Patrick's consecration to the work, St. Ninian, as we have already seen, carried the Gospel to the Southern Picts, and about the year 565, a new departure in our country's history was to be inaugurated. The instrument in producing this change was St. Columba, who then left the Monastery of Durrough, in Ireland, and launched forth in a wicker boat with twelve of his companions, full of hope and zeal for the salvation of the Western Islands and the North of Britain, where Druidism still lingered. In the Island of Iona he established his Mission with a few consecrated men of Apostolic fervour; and "from the nest of Columba," says Odonellus, "these sacred doves took their flight into all quarters," and while in others the light emitted was as that of a candle, illuminating small corners of the land, St. Columba appears before us as a mighty beacon, shin-ing out far, for the warning and guidance and salvation of men. At a time when the dark cloud was settling down upon Europe, when the progress of the race was, during what was called the middle or dark ages, under its shadowy gloom, St. Columba stands torch-bearer in front, as John de Wycliffe does at the other end, with his English Testament in his hand, the morning star of the Reformation.

CHAPTER VII.

WE now follow the current of events in our
northern part of the island. St. Ninian had
gone to his rest. The work he did was not
perpetuated. The Southern Picts, to whom he carried
the Gospel, seem to have relapsed into their original
condition. At least, much of his work seems to have
perished with him. The darkness, scattered for the
moment, closed in again, and apparently swallowed
up all. Yet, as the traditional aspects of his story
show, his life and work were by no means in vain.
It stands out indeed, as an isle of light with a night
of darkness encompassing it on every side. The
heathen Picts he started well; put them on the right
road, though they seem soon to have gone out of the
way. But perhaps their course was not so much
that of a pilgrim started well and losing the way, as
of a river descending out of sight, only to flow on in
an underground channel. The soil, to vary the meta-
phor, was probably, in consequence of the labours
of St. Ninian, in a state of preparedness for the
good seed to be sown by another; or, as a fire that had
been smouldering, and suddenly bursts forth into a

bright shining flame at the slightest breath of wind.
To the north of the Grampians was a region as yet, so
far as seen, utterly untouched by any Christian or
civilising influences. Indeed, the whole of Scotland
north of the Forth and Clyde was a dark picture.
There dwelt multitudes of wild men, grouped in tribes
or clans, whom the Romans could neither civilise nor
subdue, and who were the terror of their southern
neighbours. Here, then, was a field for heroic Christian effort—to "clear the dark places and let in the
law;" to cast out the devil and all his works, after so
long a reign, and to plant in these benighted regions
the standard of the cross. The "fulness of time" was
come, and the man was also at hand. St. Columba
was that man. He, with the sacred lamp of Divine
truth, advances to the work. Like the promise of an
unquenchable fountain to unquenchable thirst, he
suddenly emerges in our land, and stands before us
a man of massive influence. He has rough material
to work on—many difficulties to encounter. But he
consecrates himself to the work with a passionate
sense of the Infinite. The marvellous powers of his
voice have been commented on—its clear sounding
tones heard a mile off, floating along on the western
waves. His powers of organisation; the firm grip
with which he held the reins of government; the
reverent obedience accorded to him by the whole
community of which he was the head; and the altogether unparalleled success that waited on his labours:
all bespeak him a man that fitted his age "like a

glove." Other labourers in similar spheres had left the gloom unbroken except by a lamp burning feebly here and there, but Columba's labours pierced the gloom and cleared away the surrounding darkness. He rises up before us, indeed, in a setting of cloud-land, encumbered by a weight of traditions, in which the reality, in dreamlike thinness of material, loses itself in a wilderness of padding; and he looks like one of the old prophets or apostles come back to earth armed with supernatural powers. The mediæval chroniclers, whose critical powers all scholars will appraise at their true value, gathered up in one undistinguishable heap, fact and fiction, truth and error, the thing as it was, and the accretions that grew around, and modified it. They took no more care, some of them, what they were thinking about, than if their heads were channels for any rubbish to swill through that happened to be in the way. According to these literary luminaries, St. Columba prophesies, sees visions, performs miracles, cures inveterate diseases, accords safety to storm-tossed vessels, and even walks on the sea to his island home. Nay, we are told that his powers were such that " he drove demons out of milk-pails, outwitted sorcerers, and gave supernatural powers to domestic implements," and such like. But, notwithstanding these accretions of error, which have clustered round this story, the story itself is, in the main, abundantly authenticated. The tree is there, though the ivy twines round it. As we look steadily at the subject, wreath after wreath the mist

clears away, and we see revealed in the clear sun-
shine, about the year 565 A.D., this most renowned of
early Celtic missionaries, the father of the Church of
Scotland, leaving the monastery of Durrough, Ireland,
whence he set sail in a wicker boat with his companions,
animated with zeal for the conversion of the Western
Isles and Northern shores of Scotland, and the isle of
Iona, one of the smallest of the Hebrides group, only
about three miles long, and nearly a mile in breadth,
situated in the midst of "wide waters," becomes for
centuries the focus of the world's light and learning.
From it Christian missionaries, filled with enthusiastic
zeal, are despatched in all directions, carrying the
message of the Gospel to our benighted countrymen,
especially to those parts of the land that had not
been overtaken by earlier missionary efforts, and
greater works are done by these men in the conversion of our savage ancestors to Christianity, than all
the marvels with which mediæval legends have surrounded the name of St. Columba. From his sea-girt
isle, he and his companions went as far as the Orkneys, founding monasteries everywhere, on the pattern
of the parent establishment, till the whole land was
covered with a net-work of Christian agencies and
civilising influences. The Celts of Scotland and Ireland, and the Angles and Saxons in the north of
England, alike shared the "light and blessing" that
streamed from this island "retreat." Nor was the fame
of this little island confined to Britain and Ireland,
but, as already hinted, at a time when a dark cloud

of ignorance and superstition hung over Europe, its influence was felt and recognised far and wide.

The organisation of the Celtic Church thus founded in our land by St. Columba, being of a monastic character, a consideration of the origin, nature, and development of that institution, here claims something more than a mere passing notice, no less because it was in the air, and pervaded universal Christendom with its spirit, than because it entered into the genius of the Columban Church, which dominated in Scotland for centuries. The institution of Monachism was founded by St. Antony, (251-356). It was organised and reformed by St. Benedict, (480-543); and still further modified and extended by St. Francis (1182-1226). It was introduced into Africa by St. Antony and St. Augustine. Athanasius originated it at Rome and North Italy. To St. Martin of Tours, the instructor and relative of St. Ninian, is attributed its introduction to Gaul; while Pelagius, whose views were in a former lecture commented on, is said to have introduced it into Britain. The monks lived apart from the world, under Ascetic rule. Poverty, chastity, celibacy, and obedience, were their characteristics. They were divided into two classes, 1st, the Cenobites, who lived together under common discipline; and, 2nd, the Anchorites or Hermits, who lived in solitude. This system, considered as a state of religious retirement, with its accompaniments of contemplation and devotion, its ascetical and penitential practices, is not peculiar to Christianity, but has been found in several religious systems, ancient and modern,—notably in that of Judaism, of which the Essenes in the time of our Lord, are an example; while in the Fakirs of India, and the Lamas of Tibet, the same thing is observed. As an institution, then, the religious life, as seen in the conventual system, is to be referred to a general tendency or form of Oriental thought on religion which is known by the name of Asceticism. This word is used to denote the exercise and discipline practised by the athletes or wrestlers, who had to harden their bodies by exertion, and to avoid all sensual and effeminating indulgences. In the schools of the philosophers, especially the Stoics, the same word signified the practice of mastering the desires and passions, or of severe virtue. In these senses it passed into the language and thought of the early Christians. The exhortation of our Lord to voluntary poverty (Matt. xix. 21), and St. Paul's recommendation of celibacy (1 Cor. vii. 37), seemed to them to afford justification for the ascetic life. The language of St. Paul also, in comparing the Christians to wrestlers who had to contend with Satan, the world, and the flesh, contributed to the same results. But the philosophy of the time, which regarded matter as the prolific fountain of all evil, and the emancipation of mind from its bondage as the grand means of union with God, had more to do with the rise of this system. The Christians regarded the world in which they lived —the Roman Pagan world—as wicked and abominable; and they seemed to hear the voice of the

E

Master,—the "still, small voice,"—amid the noise and strife of prevailing iniquity, saying: "Come out from among them, and be ye separate, and touch not the unclean thing, and I will receive you, and will be a Father unto you, and ye shall be my sons and daughters." The Pagan world was cruel, and the fires of persecution it kindled reinforced the "still small voice," and the Christians fled to deserts, and caves, and solitary places. In the self-inflicted tortures of the Yogis and Fakirs; the suicides in the sacred Ganges and under the wheels of Juggernauth; in the offering of children in sacrifice, and the burning of widows on the funeral piles of their deceased husbands, we see asceticism in all its horrors. In the Buddhist superstition we see, in its contemning the world; in its inculcating a life of solitude and beggary; mortification of the body, and abstinence from all uncleanness and from all exciting drinks, the aim is, to keep as distant and detached as possible from this "vale of sorrow." The Egyptian Therapeutæ, who abstained from more than one wife; who exercised themselves in moderate flagellations; and whose feasts were characterised by the absence of swine's flesh and the presence of the dead, exhibited, on the whole, a form of asceticism of a comparatively mild type, like that of our modern Vegetarians and Good Templars. The joyousness of Greek life was never invaded by asceticism—though in the view of the Socratic school, which represented the body as the prison of the soul, we see a dim shadow of it crossing the field of Greek

thought ; for Stoicism and Cynicism never really reflected the popular Greek mind, which was cast essentially in the moulds of cheerfulness. The Jewish
converts to Christianity brought with them their convictions about fasting and Nazaritic observances. The
inculcations of celibacy on the early Christians, on the
ground of the expected speedy reappearance of Christ,
falls in with the same notion, namely, that the flesh,
that is, the sensuous part of our nature, is the seat of
sin, and must therefore, before all things, be rigorously
chained. The old Oriental traditions of asceticism ;
the spirituality of Christianity, pointing away from
earth to heaven ; opposition to the corruption of the
heathen world ; the distinction made between belief
and knowledge, as a higher and lower stage of intelligence leading to a corresponding distinction of a
higher and lower stage of virtue—all combined to
make the Christians of the first three centuries hold
aloof from the world and its ways, and favour the
celibate life. Virgins wore veils and mitres of purple
and gold to indicate that none need apply to them to
propose marriage, as they were wedded to the Church.
And to such an extent did this ascetic spirit obtain,
that, early in the second century, the perilous practice
of men and women living together under vows of con-
tinence was in vogue. A very violent recoil from this
custom was early witnessed in the rule by which the
sexes were separated in the conventual system, no
male being allowed to enter the precincts of a nun-
nery, and *vice versa*. On this point it is not a little

ludicrous to observe the principle carried out even in regard to the lower animals, and to find, in the establishments on Mount Athos in Greece, a rule by which all female animals were rigorously excluded from the sacred precincts of the Monasteries. But during the first three centuries no irrevocable vows yet bound the devotees to a life-long asceticism. At first the Christians thought it sufficient to absent themselves from all heathen festivals and amusements; but by and by extreme views crept in connected with a belief in the merit of celibacy, of abstinence from particular kinds of food, of self-inflicted tortures, etc. And whereas at first the solitary life was looked upon as only a refuge to which they were driven by persecution or prevailing ungodliness, afterwards the glory of a life spent in loneliness and austerity became a substitute for that of the martyr's death. The hermits first left the cities for the villages and rural districts, then betook themselves to the desert and outlying solitudes, far from the society of men. One sect of them, called Boskoi, grazed with the common herds in the fields of Mesopotamia. They dwelt in caves and in cages. They wore chains and iron rings, and through many years maintained painful postures. A somewhat startling development of asceticism is seen in the Pillar Saints, a form of superstition that existed in the East—principally in Syria—from the 5th to the 12th century. Simeon the Stylite, a monk of the 5th century, stands at the head of this movement. Of him we read that, for nine years, he

lived in a monastery without ever moving from his
cell; that, increasing in enthusiasm, he withdrew to a
place 40 miles from Antioch, where he erected a pillar
on the top of which, only a yard in diameter, he took
up his position—a position of most complete separa-
tion from the earth. From this he removed to several
others in succession, each higher than the previous
one, till he attained to one of 40 cubits in height.
On the top of those pillars he spent 37 years of his
life, his neck loaded with an iron chain, and his
lips in constant prayer; and during his more overt
acts of devotion he bent his body so that his fore-
head touched his feet. His powers of fasting have
also been noted. He frequently limited himself to
a single meal in the week. If we are to believe the
traditional accounts regarding this phase of his
life, he fasted during the 40 days of Lent with an
entire abstinence from food. In consequence of
these austerities, his fame was such that crowds of
pilgrims from distant countries, even from Britain,
came to see him; and many Pagans and Saracens, we
are told, were converted by looking up to the saint on
his pillar, as the Israelites were healed when they
looked at the serpent of brass. Of one of his disciples
we read that for 33 years he maintained this mode of
life in the more trying climate of the shores of the
Bosphorus, four miles from Constantinople, where
sometimes he was almost blown from the top of his
pillar by the storms of Thrace, and for days he was
covered with snow and ice. The earliest form of the

ascetic life was that of the hermit who lived in solitary retirement from the world; but in course of time the devotees came to be grouped together in cells, with a common sanctuary to which they might repair to nourish the religious life. The little cluster of cells round a common place of worship was called a *Laura*, an institution which bridged the gap, and formed the transition between the Eremitic and the Cenobitic forms of Monachism, and arose out of a deep-seated want of our nature which the solitary life of the hermit did not satisfy. That want can only be met in the public worship of God. The lonely recluse in his desert cave had entered into David's experience when he said:—"When I remember these things, I pour out my soul in me; for I had gone with the multitude: I went with them to the House of God, with the voice of joy and praise, with a multitude that kept holiday." Psalms xlii. 4. It was in the Cenobitic, rather than the Eremitic form that Monachism was first introduced into the west. As already observed, St. Anthony (251-356) was its founder. He found Asceticism in the air. He consolidated and crowned it by the institution of the monastic system. In Upper Egypt this father of Monachism was born. A man of great wealth, he sold his possessions, and distributed them to the poor. He withdrew himself from the society of his fellows into a wilderness, where he practised his austerities. Then, penetrating into the far interior, he fixed his residence in an old ruin on the top of a hill. Afterwards he founded the

Monastery of Faioum, a group of separate and
scattered cells, near Memphis. This was the origin of
the Cenobite life. The persecution of the Christians
by Maximian, in 311 A.D., induced him to leave his
cell and go to Alexandria, in the hope of obtaining the
crown of martyrdom. Failing in this, he plunged
deeper into the desert, till he settled down in a place
about a day's journey from the Red Sea, and became
the mighty oracle of the Nile. In the year 355 A.D.,
when 104 years of age, we find the venerable hermit
making his way to Alexandria, this time to dispute
with the Arian heretics. Here he meets Athanasius,
the great champion of orthodoxy in that heretical age.
Feeling his end approaching, Antony retired to his
desert home, where he died at the advanced age of
105 years, to become, as he well deserved, the most
popular Saint in the Romish Calendar. It is easy to
laugh at this institution; and truly, in some of its
aspects, the Monastic life presented quite a ludicrous
appearance. But it well becomes us to judge charit-
ably of those who thus surrendered wealth, pleasure,
home, and friends, at the bidding of duty and loyalty
to Christ. It is easy for a professing Protestant, who
never experienced the friction of a noble heart-sur-
render to God and duty, to asperse the character of
those who lived the ascetic life by attributing to them
heretical views of doctrine and selfish views of morals.
But let those who thus judge exhibit a similar devotion to the cause of Christ, and then they will be
entitled to a hearing. Meanwhile it becomes all to

remember that it is not the "hearers of the law," but the "doers" that are justified. In the dark ages, the monasteries were abodes of light. They were the centres of secular learning and Christian culture. The monks of the middle ages were perhaps the best preachers that ever existed. They issued from their cells, like men inspired, and, with flashes of fervid eloquence, electrified their hearers. "The monasteries were quiet havens amid surrounding tempests. Amid the terrible insecurity of life, and the utter disregard of right and wrong, which we can discern to have been characteristics of Heathenism, here was comparative security; here were truth and righteousness." But for them the treasures of antiquity, both sacred and secular, would have perished. No man who rightly estimates the value of those records in which the sacred tradition has been preserved to our time, can refuse to recognise in that institution in which the transcription of ancient manuscripts was carried on and the richly-freighted raft floated down the ages, one of the most beneficent, and in the providence of God, one of the wisest possible arrangements. The Christian who sees in the superstition of the Jews in regard to the letter of Scripture a guarantee of the purity of the text, will naturally be led to thank God for the past existence of such superstition as led a copyist of the cloister to append to his work the following attestation of authenticity, a form which was typical as found in numerous manuscripts: "This book, copied by M. N., for the benefit of his soul, was finished in the year——. May the Lord think upon him !" Every man, then, who values the Bible may well rejoice that such an institution existed in times when all Europe was in a state of turmoil and dis-organisation. It is thus due to Monachism that we are able to traverse the gulf of general ignorance that separates the intelligence and civilisation of antiquity from modern times, and to land on the native soil of these monuments of mind, and memorials of the foun-dation of our Scottish Church.

CHAPTER VIII.

IN my last sketch I gave a bird's eye view of the character and work of Columba, and of the monastic system on which his organisation was founded. Among the world's great men he is entitled to no mean place. Head and shoulders above the greatest of his contemporaries, he is the leading figure on the canvas of the 6th century, in which he strides like a colossus, as a great social fact, contributing in large measure to shape the destinies of men, and to form fresh channels, broad and deep, for the stream of national progress to flow down the ages. An epoch man like him is one of the great bulwarks of history ; a mirror in which we see reflected the age and body of the time ; a clue to the inner meaning of the facts of history in their relations to the past and present: "As I take it," says Carlyle, "universal history, the history of what man has accomplished in this world is at the bottom the history of the great men who have worked here. They were the leaders of men, these great ones; the modellers, patterns, and, in a

wide sense, creators of whatsoever the general mass of
men contrived to do or to attain; all things that we
see standing accomplished in the world are properly
the outer material result, the practical realisation and
embodiment of thoughts that dwelt in the great men
sent into the world. . . . The great man is the
living light-fountain which it is good and pleasant to
be near. The light which enlightens, which has enlightened the darkness of the world; and this not as
a kindled lamp only, but rather as a natural luminary
shining by the gift of heaven; a flowing light-fountain, as I say, of native original insight, of manhood
and heroic nobleness; in whose radiance all souls feel
that it is well with them. On any terms whatsoever
you will not grudge to wander in such neighbourhood
for a while." A brief survey of the facts of Columba's
life must here suffice. He was born at Gartan, in the
County of Donegal, in the north of Ireland, on the 7th
of December, 521 A.D. His father, Fedhlimidh, was a
kinsman of more than one chief then reigning in Ireland and the west of Scotland. His mother, Eithne,
was also of royal descent. He studied under St.
Finnian at Clonard, where there was a monastery of
3000 monks; a great training school of missionaries.
St. Finnian had twelve chief disciples, who filled the
land with religious settlements. Columba was one of
this chosen band. Among his fellow-disciples he is
supposed to have had St. Comgall, St. Ciaran, and St.
Cainnech, a triumvirate of luminaries; and so conspicuous was his youthful devotion, even in that

saintly company, that he received the name by which
he is still best known in Ireland, "Columcille," or
"Columba of the Cell," hence, too, the common name
of the Island of Iona, "I-columkill," "the Island of
Colum of the Cells." In 546 A.D. Columba founded
Derry, and six or seven years afterwards Durrow, the
greatest of all his Irish monasteries, of which the
number was considerable. Of these monastic colleges
St. Patrick and his disciples founded about a hundred,
and such was their celebrity, that, as Bede informs us,
the youths of Britain were sent to them for education.
One of the most celebrated of these monasteries was
at Bangor, in Down, of which St. Comgall was the
first Abbot. This establishment is said to have contained 3000 residents. Another, equally eminent, was
that of St. Finnian at Clonard, near the Boyne, in
which, as we have already noted, Columba for some
time studied. St. Ciaran, whose cave and chapel are
pointed out near Campbeltown, and whose virtues
have been summed up in the saying that "he never
told a lie, nor looked upon a woman," was also the
father and founder of one at Clon, upon the Shenan;
while Cainnech, the saint of Kilkenny, founded a
monastery in the eastern corner of Fife, at a spot by
the sea called Rig Monadh, the royal mount, the scene
of the great church and monastery of St. Andrew's,
hence anciently called Kilrymont. In these institutions we see the embryo of our cathedrals and
universities in later times. They were so many
colleges of learned divines whereunto the people

usually resorted for instruction, and the Church was
wont continually to be supplied with able ministers.
No wonder the Irish love to dwell with such enthusiastic delight upon these times, when we find them
sending forth such holy men as Columba, the founder
of Iona; Columbanus, the founder of monasteries in
France and Italy; Cœlius Sedulius, Aidan, Finan,
Gallus, and others, some of whom laboured so successfully among the Anglo Saxons in the seventh century.
In the beginning of the ninth century there were no
fewer than 7000 students in the single college of
Ardmagh (Armagh), notwithstanding that there were
three more (Cashel, Dundaleathglass, and Lismore)
which vied with this, besides a great many private
and independent training institutions in other parts
of the island. For, "let it be remembered," as it has
been well said, "that there was a time when Ireland
was the sanctuary of Christian truth, the school of
Europe, the nurse and the mother of the holiest men,
and the enlightener of an age of darkness. Upon
this period a cloud has hitherto rested, enveloping it
in the profoundest obscurity. Its most heroic and
saintly names have been dealt with as the shadows of
a myth. The memory of it has been preserved in our
days only by a few faint allusions to it in authors of
more than ordinary research. No traveller visits
Ireland with the thought that he is treading ground
hallowed and ennobled as one of the brightest sanctuaries of the Church. He looks upon its bordered
castles and ruined abbeys, numerous as they are, con-

temptuously, as compared with the grander monuments of England, and painfully, as associated only
with records of turbulence and crime. A Danish rath
or a Druidical stone may catch his attention for a
moment; a slight question may cross his mind as to
the reality of a St. Patrick, or the school of St.
Columba; but to look for any trace of their footsteps,
or any light upon their history, would seem a delusion
like a struggle to exhume the relics of a pre-adamite
nation." How bright with promise was Ireland then,
how sad its condition now! How has its golden age
been succeeded by one of brass? A star in the
literary world lately set has said: "The honesty of
the Greeks begins at what is the hanging point with
us." And to such a level has that unhappy country
sunk, that in crime and ignorance, in murder and
robbery, it bids fair to vie with the reputation of the
Greeks. It is enough to overlay all human hope and
enterprise with an eternal frost, to think that the
ground which was trodden then by Christian heroes,
the excellent of the earth, is now crawled over by
those swarms of men who preach a gospel of hatred
and robbery. Poor Ireland! a brighter future, let us
hope, awaits her; but at present the darkness thickens;
the light grows less. Then Christianity was a living
power, quickening the heart and ennobling the life;
now it is but a name, and scarcely penetrates skin
deep! "Most of these men," says Fuller, "seem born
under a travelling planet, seldom having their education in the place of their nativity; oft-times composed

of Irish infancy, British breeding, and French prefer-
ment; taking a cowl in one country, a crozier in
another, and a grave in a third; neither bred where
born, nor beneficed where bred, nor buried where
beneficed; but wandering in several kingdoms." The
reason which determined Columba to leave Ireland,
where he bulked so largely in that age of heroes, is
supposed to have had a political origin. He appears
to have embroiled himself in the civil strifes of his
country. A bloody battle fought in Connaught, in
561 A.D., was believed to be traceable to the action of
Columba, who was forthwith excommunicated by an
Irish ecclesiastical Synod. The justice of the sentence
was indeed challenged by ecclesiastics of rank; but
the die was cast. In 563 A.D., when in his 42nd year,
he finally took his departure from his native land, and
settled in the Island of Iona. The first temples in
which Christianity was enshrined in our island were
of the humblest description, being built of oaken
planks, or of wattles, thatched with reeds, or covered
with sheets of lead. St. Patrick, we are told, on one
occasion, built a quadrangular church of moist earth,
because wood was not near at hand. In such rude
structures did our fathers worship God when the
Pagan gods of Rome had costly temples erected in
their honour. And when Roman palaces and walls
and aqueducts were built of solid masonry, the early
Christians had in Glastonbury, "the beginning and
fountain of all religion in England," nothing more im-
posing for their oratory than a wattled hut. The

Church of St. Ninian, as already noted, marks an epoch in ecclesiastical architecture, when stone was introduced to supersede the wattled walls and reed roofs which characterised the buildings of that age in this land, when walls of twigs wended and twisted together were thought fit as well for the worship of God as for the residence of kings. At Glastonbury, where Christianity in Britain first had a "local habitation and a name," we might have expected something better. Some of the earliest transactions of the Romans took place here, and their presence here continued to the latest period of their occupation of this country. Various traces of Roman roads may be detected in different places, all pointing to the spot, and many Roman coins have been turned up within the old abbey enclosure, which covers 60 acres of land. According to a "strong and unvarying tradition," this was the scene of the first mission establishment of Christianity that was planted in Britain. It was accordingly styled in very early times "The Mother of the Saints," and by some "The Burying-place of the Saints." It became the most magnificent abbey in the world, and was guarded by the most scrupulous care, no man, be he prince or bishop, being permitted to enter its sacred precincts without leave of the Abbot, a functionary who sat among the Barons of England for 600 years. And yet this scene of hallowed memories and sacred associations consisted of a few wattled huts surrounded by a marsh, and occasionally covered with water from the tides of the

Bristol Channel. We need not, therefore, be surprised to find a similar rudeness of form in the structures reared by Columba for his establishment at Iona. The general character of the Culdee establishments is well known. There was the earthen rampart enclosing the settlement, the barn, the mill stream, the kiln, the refectory. The Church, with the sacristy, was of oak. The cells of the brethren were of clay, held together by wattles. Columba, the Abbot, had his special cell at Iona, in which he wrote and read. Like Jacob of old, he slept on the bare ground, with a stone for his pillow. The dress of the brethren was simple, and free from all adornment. It consisted of a white tunic, over which was worn a rough mantle and hood of wool of its natural colour. They bore the special tonsure—sign of the solemn vows by which the members of the community were bound—which left the forepart of the head bare. They were shod with sandals, which they took off at meals. Their food was simple also, consisting commonly of barley bread, milk, fish and eggs, with seals flesh, though on Sundays and festivals the fare was somewhat better. The training and probation of the Culdees were marked by severity of discipline and protracted study. Many of the students employed themselves in the mechanical arts, as well as in the study of medical and other sciences. The laws and customs and histories of nations, the study of the classics of antiquity, formed the groundwork of those literary pursuits which fitted the inmates of these establishments for their great

F

work as pioneers of civilisation in this land, and re-
storers of it in others where it was in decline.
Attendance at public prayers three times during each
day, and as often in the night, was enjoined on the
brethren.   In each office of the day they were to use
prayers, and chant three psalms; and in the offices of
the night, from October to February, they were to
chant thirty-six psalms and twelve anthems, at three
several times: through the rest of the year twenty-
one psalms and eight anthems; but on Saturdays and
Sundays twenty-five psalms and as many anthems.
Thus trained through a long period of probation,—
sometimes, as in the case of St. Munn, extending over
eighteen years,—Iona sent forth her missionaries into
this and other lands, from which ignorance and idolatry were to be banished by the influence of Christian
civilisation.   The brethren were divided into three
classes: the seniors, the working brothers (who were
exempted from the Psalter exercises), and the pupils.
In the most plain and frugal manner, then, did these
Culdees live, supporting themselves by the labour of
their hands.   They fasted on Wednesdays and Fridays
in Lent.   They lived a life of rule and constant self-
denial.   A peculiar form of austerity practised by
some was to remain in cold water till they had
repeated the entire Psalter.   The chief service was
the Communion, celebrated each Sunday and on all
festal days.   Easter—which they celebrated at a
different time from the rest of Christendom, because,
as Bede says, "In that far-out-of-the-world abode of

theirs, none had ever communicated to them the synodal decrees relating to the Paschal observance "— was the great festival of their Christian year. If we look at the outside of this establishment at Iona, we see little to satisfy our æsthetical feelings in the little group of mud and wattled huts, and in the austere life of the brethren who found in these cells sanctuaries, under whose low roofs high thoughts were wont to dwell. The island itself, with its "picturesque bays, quiet dells, green hills, and plains not unfruitful," presents yet little that is strikingly attractive to the lover of natural scenery ; and then, when its social gloom was unbroken by the light of woman's smile, it seems like a desolation—a place enveloped by weird mists. For these monks were strict celibates, and on this consecrated island no woman was allowed to land. The poet Otway has said :—

> " O woman ! lovely woman ! Nature made thee
> To temper man ; we had been brutes without you."

But this fanciful eulogium of woman on the background of so unimposing a view of man can scarcely apply to the Culdee establishments of Columba, for on this foil of asceticism we see set a faith, like the rainbow in the cloud, reflecting a bright lustre on the scene ; a service training souls to a life of high consecration to the highest interests of man. The outcome of this organisation and life of rule was fraught with the beneficence of the Gospel of Christ. The poor were the especial objects on which the brethren bestowed their care. The hungry had their wants supplied; the sick were carefully tended; and the ignorant were taken up and instructed by these saintly men. St. Aidan, for instance, had the charge of twelve children, to whom he was to be a "nursing father," feeding, clothing, and educating them as his own. From this centre of Christian nurture there radiated in all directions lines of light. Swarms of missionaries hived off from this parent establishment, and settled at various points, amid a great surrounding heathen population, in which they formed so many Christian colonies. They went out day by day, labouring in various places with zeal and boldness in the work of the Master, and at night they repaired to their cloistered retreat, where, amid the companionship of the brethren, they found the comfort and refreshment which, in such circumstances, human nature so urgently needs. Wherever these centres were established, there was a zone of cultivated land reclaimed from the morass and the forest, a significant symbol of the character of the influence wielded by these Culdee missionaries on surrounding spiritual barrenness and heathen growths. Their first religious house of any importance on the mainland was at Abernethy, the Church of which is said to have been built in Columba's lifetime, and which became the principal seat of royalty in the Pictish Kingdom. St. Andrew's also was a foundation of the Culdees, as well as Dunkeld, Dumblane, Brechin, and other places. As to the mode in which Columba carried on his operations in the evangelising of this land we know little. Adam-

nan, his biographer, and one of his successors, extols
his wonderful powers, and relates how, on one occasion, he arrived at the Pictish king's fort, the gates
suddenly burst open at his approach; and how, as he
chanted the 45th Psalm, his voice, always loud and
deep, was preternaturally strengthened so as to be
heard like a thunder-peal above the din and clamour
by which the magicians tried to silence his evening
prayer under the walls of the Pictish palace. A Celtic
manuscript of a later date records how Columba and a
disciple came from Hy (Iona) to Aberdour, a beautiful
little bay among the huge cliffs which fringe the coast
of Buchan; how Bede, a Pict, was then high-steward
of Buchan, and "gave them that town in freedom for
evermore." In some such way as this Columba seems
to have traversed the Pictish mainland, the Western
Islands, and the Orkneys, establishing humble monasteries whose inmates ministered to the religious wants
of the people. Thirty-four years of his life were spent
in this way, during which time he converted the Pictish king Brude, who dwelt at the mouth of the river
Ness, not far from the modern town, Inverness. And
when Aidan succeeded Columba's cousin Connal, king
of the Scots, he was crowned by Columba at Iona—
the first Christian coronation of our Scottish kings.
He paid repeated visits to his old home, Ireland, where
he was still much beloved. And when Glasgow was
still unborn, he visited St. Kentigern or Mungo, its
father and patron saint, who was then engaged preaching Christianity among the Welsh or British tribes of

Cumbria and Strathclyde. The health of Columba began to fail in the year 593 A.D., when he was in his 72nd year, though his life was prolonged till he reached his 77th year. When his end was approaching, he visited the working brethren on the opposite side of the island to that on which the monastery was situated. From the litter in which he was carried he addressed them in gentle tones, which made them sad, as they thought of the inevitable stroke which was so soon to descend on him who was their father and head. Turning to the east, he blessed the island and all its inhabitants, as from the verge of the shores of all-subduing time. A week afterwards he felt that his last day on earth had dawned. It was a Saturday, the 8th day of June. With his faithful attendant, Diormit, he went to bless the barn; and rejoiced to think that there was provision enough for his beloved Monks for a year. "This day," he said, "in the holy Scriptures, is called the Sabbath, which means rest, and this day is indeed a Sabbath to me, for it is the last day of my present laborious life, and on it I rest after the fatigues of my labours; and this night at midnight, which commenceth the solemn Lord's Day, I shall go the way of our fathers. For already my Lord Jesus Christ deigneth to invite me; and to Him in the middle of this night I shall depart at His invitation. For so it hath been revealed to me by the Lord Himself." Returning to the monastery, we are told, that a white horse that used to carry the milk vessels from the cowshed to the dairy came to the saint, and laying its head on his breast, began to shed tears of distress. The poor man blest his humble fellow-creature; then, ascending the hill hard by, he looked upon the monastery, and, holding up his hands, breathed his last benediction upon the place he had ruled so well. Arrived at his little hut, he took up, for the last time, his task of transcribing the Psalter. The last lines he wrote are the 8th and 9th verses of the 34th Psalm:—"O taste and see that the Lord is good; blessed is the man that trusteth in Him. O fear the Lord, ye His saints; for there is no want to them that fear Him." This done, he laid down his pen for the last time, saying: "Here, at the end of the page, I must stop: let Baithene write what comes after." At evening service he was present; and, amid the sighing of the wind and the moaning of the sea, he lifted up his voice in prayer and praise. After service he returned to his chamber, lay down on his bed—a bare flag—and from his stony pillow he gave his last counsels to the brethren, in words breathing peace and charity. Then, subsiding into silence, he lay till the midnight bell rung in the Lord's Day, when he rose and entered the church in haste, followed by his attendant. There was the saint alone, kneeling before the altar; and to the eyes of the advancing brethren, the whole church was ablaze with heavenly light; but, as they entered, the light vanished and all was dark. When lights were brought the saint was lying before the altar. With a countenance lighted up with joy and peace, he looked eagerly to right and left, moved his right hand in blessing on his brethren; and thus the wearied saint passed to his rest, amid the lamentations of the monks. For three days and nights, a storm of wind and rain beat upon the island; but the sea grew calm when the saint was laid in his lowly bed to his last sleep.

CHAPTER IX.

THE elements of civilisation, for which we are
mainly indebted to the Romans, affected first
the southern parts of Britain, and were long
rigorously excluded from the wilds of Caledonia. But
in process of time, in language and literature, in architecture and improved agriculture, the Roman civilisation penetrated those parts which were inaccesible to
their arms. And Christianity, the greatest blessing
of all, was first imported hither during the Roman
occupation. In tracing the foundations of the Celtic
Church, our attention was first drawn to South Britain, where it took its rise. Early in the fourth century, under Constantine, Christianity became the
religion of the State. In the fifth century St. Ninian
established himself at *Candida Casa*, and laboured for
the conversion of the southern Picts; and a century
later St. Columba, from his monastery at Iona, spread
a network of Christian agencies north of the Grampians. Before taking up the thread of the story from
the life and labours of St. Columba, I propose to forecast a little, by introducing to you in outline a view
of what is known as Mediævalism, at the threshold of

which we now find ourselves. I shall then invite you to look a little ahead, to see what is going on in the political and social state of this country during the next few centuries in which the Columban Church flourished, and conclude with a brief account of the life and labours of St. Kentigern. Thus, by keeping up our acquaintance with the outside world, by letting in side-lights from the development of the Christian system in Europe, and by tracing the progress of Christianity in connection with our social and political advancement; by, as it were, throwing over the subject the social sky of evolution, we may hope to arrive at a juster conception than would be possible in any isolated treatment of our theme. The period at which we have now arrived was one of much interest. Politically, confusion and darkness reigned; wave after wave had passed over the surface of the old Roman State, and obliterated almost all the landmarks of the ancient time. But in the general dissolution that followed the dismemberment of the old Empire, in the confusion that followed the decay of the old order of things, the Church was rising into prominence. The monks gathered up and saved from ruin whatever was valuable and capable of assimilation. They rescued agriculture from neglect, and preserved the monuments of ancient learning. In times of turbulence and bloodshed, these men were secure as within walls of adamant. A religious reverence proved a surer safeguard to these men than castles or armour could have been. No marauder dare trespass on lands under the protection of priest and bishop. The storms that raged outside produced no ripple on the calm life of religious meditation within the cloister. Over the chaos of contending powers appeared the mitre and crozier of the Pope. A combination of many agencies we see for ages at work in weaving that fine and curious network which, at first no bigger than a man's hand, was stretched further and wider, till it became "a covering spread over all nations," including and confining within its fatal meshes the bodies and the souls of men. We are now bordering on the middle ages, that strange bridge across the gulf that separates ancient and modern history. All Europe we see with its night-cap on, composing itself to sleep ; and, while the dark cloud creeps over the sky, sleeping soundly. During the long night of the dark ages, that "parenthesis," as it has been called, in the history of the human mind, which, preceded and followed by bright days, seems all the more gloomy by the contrast, we see the decline of learning going on side by side with the rise and growth of the Papal power. The popularity the Church attained from its beneficent action in times of lawlessness and injustice, brought with it temptations from which poverty or unpopularity would have kept it free. As it gained in power it sank in morals. It was in the decay of learning that the Papal power advanced, as it was when men slept that "the enemy sowed his tares." During that long night, which may roughly be said to extend from the seventh to the fourteenth century, the human intellect was wrapt in a profound slumber. We look in vain for learning or original genius. One or two figures now and then flit across the darkness, as one meets an occasional belated townsman in the deserted streets of the city at midnight. St. Columba and St. Kentigern stand out from the crowd, when the cloud was settling down on the world, as the foremost men of their day, holding the torch of Christianity in front of the advancing night. Scotus Erigena and Alfred the Great emerge, when the night was at its darkest, holding in their hands the lantern of philosophy in the midst of the surrounding gloom; and John de Wycliffe, with his English Bible, appears in early dawn, when the cloud is passing away, the herald of the Renaissance—the "Morning Star" of the Reformation.

In looking at the map of Scotland,—at this time called Alban, or Pictland, or Caledonia,—we have to remember that it was divided into four kingdoms, two in the region north of the Forth, and two south of that estuary. In the north, Alban proper, were the Picts and the Scots, the former in the east and the latter in the west; while southward of that line were, on the west, the Britons of Strathclyde; and on the east the Saxons of Northumbria. From Ireland, the land of the Scots, then called Scotia, a colony had settled in Argyleshire in the 5th century. At first over-shadowed by the more powerful monarchy of the Picts, they gradually increased in numbers and strength, till, in the 9th century, by a revolution, the

Scots acquired a predominance in northern Britain. Their first prince, Fergus, came to Britain early in the 6th century. His great-grandson, Conal, was king of the Scots when Columba began his great work, the conversion of the northern Picts. Aidan, his nephew, who was crowned by Columba at Iona, was a powerful prince ; but his successors were obscure. During these reigns almost all we know of the Scots is that they were in unceasing conflict with the Picts, as well as with the Britons of Cumbria. In the year 836 Kenneth M'Alpine succeeded his father as king of the Scots. He was lineal descendant of Fergus and Aidan. The Pictish kingdom, weakened by civil dissension and a disputed claim to the throne, was easily won over by Kenneth, who laid claim to it as the true heir in the female line. In 843 Kenneth became king of the united kingdom of the Picts and Scots. The first Christian king of the Picts was Brude, the son of Mailcon, whom Bede styles a very powerful king. His chief residence was on the banks of the Ness, and there Columba baffled and confuted his heathen magicians. Of the successors of Brude, engaged, for the most part, in war with their Northumbrian and Scot neighbours, we select two as worthy of mention here. The first is Nectan, son of Dereli, who succeeded about the year 710. He cultivated learning to some extent, and aspired to the position of an ecclesiastical reformer. Like our own James VI., he took part in ecclesiastical councils. At one which he summoned to discuss the questions of ritual and Easter, he endea-

voured to carry out a policy to assimilate these observances in Scotland to the English model. In a letter
from the Abbot of Jarrow, whom he consulted in this
and other matters, and which appears in the works of
Bede, he is thus addressed:—" To the most excellent
lord, and most glorious King Nectan." The king's
command was peremptory; the Scottish Church was
to be overshadowed by the English. Architects were
sent by the Abbot of Jarrow to build a church of
stone in the Roman fashion, which he proposed to
dedicate to St. Peter. The Scots were unmoved by
his authoritative commands. His policy was post-
poned for four centuries, and St. Andrew was destined
to keep his ground against St. Peter. But the most
active of all the Pictish sovereigns was Hungus, son
of Urgust, who succeeded in 730, and reigned for 30
years. He was engaged in constant wars with the
Scots, the Britons, and the English, in which he was
generally victorious. After his death the kingdom of
the Picts suffered rapid decline, its latest period being
involved in impenetrable obscurity. All that we know
for certain is the final result. Various princes claimed
the crown, and held possession of various portions of
the kingdom, till Kenneth, king of Scots, the most
powerful competitor, was acknowledged king, and
fixed his residence at Forteviot in Strathern, the
then capital of the Pictish Kingdom.

The name of Scotland was first given to the United
Kingdom of the Picts and Scots in the tenth century,
superseding the ancient names of Pictavia, or Pictland,

Alban, or Caledonia, by which it had formerly been known. The Picts and Scots now gradually coalesced into one people, whose territory extended from the Friths of Forth and Clyde to the northern extremity of Britain. While St. Ninian had taught Christianity among the Picts south of the Grampians, and St. Columba in his labours overtook the region north of that boundary, the country south of the Forth, inhabited by the Strathclyde Britons, was not left in darkness. Early in the sixth century there arose one who, contemporary with Columba, made his mark on that age; and, in the City of Glasgow, of which he may be called the Father, we recognise a monument erected to his memory, and a type of his enduring fame. St. Kentigern (A.D. 516-601), or, as he is more popularly named, St. Mungo, or the beloved, a title which speaks of the amiability of his character, was connected with the royal family of the Cumbrian Britons through his mother, St. Thenau. He was educated at Culross by St. Serf, who had a cell there, an educational establishment whose fame was widespread, as a centre of Christianity whose light irradiated the north shore of the Firth of Forth. After being educated at this school, he planted a small religious establishment on the banks of a little stream which falls into the Clyde at what is now the city of Glasgow. Upon a tree beside the clearing in the forest he hung his bell, to summon the savage people of the neighbourhood to worship, and the tree with the bell still appears in the arms of Glasgow. Thus

was the commencement made of what in time became
a seat of population in connection with a Culdee
establishment; by and bye an industrious town; ulti-
mately, what we may now see, a magnificent city with
more than a half a million of inhabitants. In the
midst of his great work troubles came upon him. The
king of the Strathclyde Britons was his enemy, and
made the place so hot for him that he fled for refuge
to Wales, where, however, he did not relax his efforts
as a Christian Missionary. At Menevia, now St.
David's, he found a congenial friend and brother in
the saintly David, whose name is perpetuated in that
See. Under David the cause of religion attained to
great prosperity. "He was to all," says Giraldus, "A
mirror and a pattern of life; he taught both by pre-
cept and example; was an excellent preacher in words,
but more excellent in works. He was a doctrine to
those who heard him, a model to the religious, life to
the needy, defence to orphans, support to widows, a
father to the fatherless, a rule to works, a directory to
men of the world; being made all things to all men,
that he might win all to God." During St. Kentigern's residence in Wales, between 540 and 560, a
religious Prince of Denbighshire bestowed upon him a
piece of land at the confluence of the rivers Elwy and
Clwyd, on which he built a school and monastery,
called from it Llan-Elwy, where a great number of
disciples and scholars soon placed themselves under
his direction. His enemy of Strathclyde being now
dead, he, in 560, returned to his old charge in Scot-

land, whither he carried along with him many of his
scholars. On leaving Wales he appointed Asaph or
Hassaph, one of his disciples, his successor in the
school and monastery. His successor was a native of
North Wales, and his name is handed down to our
day in the See of St. Asaph. Though his old friend,
St. David, had been dead for many years, on his return
from Wales he was visited by St. Columba at his little
church beside the Clyde. One circumstance connected
with this visit is recorded. The two chief shepherds
interchanged their respective pastoral staves, as a
token of brotherly affection. St. Kentigern's pastoral
staff was not gilded and gemmed, but of simple wood,
and merely bent, and in this exchange of croziers,
unless Columba's was a very poor one, he must have
had the best of the bargain. Of St. Columba's self-
denial and austerity I have already spoken. It was
the pervading influence and spirit of the age, so far as
Christianity was concerned. It was all of this ascetic
type. St. Kentigern was by no means free from it.
In his hand he always carried his Manual Book, ready
to exercise his ministry whenever needful. His bed
was a hollow stone, in which he cast a few ashes when
he lay down. This done, taking off his sackcloth, he
wooed sleep in the ashes, like another Jacob, with a
pillow of stone for his head. "Verily," says his biographer, Joceline, "he was a staunch combatant
against the flesh, the world, and the devil." At the
second cock-crowing he arose, and, stripping himself
of his raiment, he plunged into the cold and rapid

G

stream, and then, with eyes and hands lifted up to Heaven, he chanted on end the whole Psalter. Such bodily ablutions, we are told, produced in him a wonderful physique; and we are not surprised to learn that his spirit, thus soaked in asceticism, became pure and bright, and that sometimes, when he said the *Sursum Corda*, and sought to lift up his own heart to Christ, a "glory gleamed upon his face and form, so that he seemed like a pillar of fire." For a while he abode in Dumfriesshire, where Rederech (Roderick) the Liberal, the friendly king who succeeded his enemy, met him, but Glasgow was his seat. From this centre his influence extended north as far as the Orkneys and South to Wales. Galloway also shared in his beneficent influence. Tradition assigns him a long life, 185 years. From this we may safely deduct 100 years, and say that, though he died at the age of 85, he lives through the ages, and will live not merely in those localities in which his name is known, but in those streams of holy influence which are part of our inheritance from the past, and of which he contributed so largely towards the initial impulse. In the cemetery of his church "for a long time," says his biographer, "all the great men of that region have been in the custom of being buried." There rested in old days 665 saints of God. It is still, as in days of old, customary to bury hard by the place where so many of Christ's saints sleep. And in a solemn burying-place, that awes one by its wide extent, "with terraced walks, and green slopes, and rocky graves, a very city

of the dead, the good and wise of the vast city of the
living, and many of its fair and young no less, are
laid, as of old, beneath the shadow of the great Church
of St. Kentigern." The miracles which he was believed to have wrought were so deeply rooted in the
popular mind, that some of them sprung up again in
the eighteenth century to grace the legends of the
Cameronian martyrs. Others are still commemorated
by the armorial ensigns of the city of Glasgow—a
hazel tree whose frozen branches he kindled into a
flame, a tame robin which he restored to life, a hand-
bell which he brought from Rome, a salmon which he
rescued from the depths of the Clyde, the lost ring of
the frail Queen of Cadzow. Nor is it St. Kentigern
(Mungo) only whose memory survives at Glasgow, the
Parish Church of St. Enoch commemorates his mother,
St. Thenau, and it is not many years since a neighbouring spring, which still bears her name, ceased to
be an object of occasional pilgrimage.

CHAPTER X.

WE have seen how Christianity was introduced
and extended in this land—how St. Ninian,
St. Columba, and St. Kentigern, "prepared
the way of the Lord" among the savage races that
then peopled North Britain; how St. Columba planted
religious establishments among the Picts and Scots,
and St. Kentigern Christianised the Britons of Strathclyde. Our country, thus possessed by Celtic Missionaries, the coadjutors and successors of these great men,
we can but dimly imagine the struggle which for generations must have been carried on before the Pagan
ideas gave place to Christianity in the minds of our
ancestors. It is all but impossible to place ourselves
in the position of these men—to see things as they
saw them. The effect is nothing less than an endea-
vour to revert to a ruder type of mental structure; to
put aside our hereditary culture, and to become for
the time barbarians. The distance between eastern
and western thought, the interval that separates the
European from the Asiatic mind, is a faint approxima-
tion of the contrast between the Christianity of a
Columba or Benedict, and the heathenism of one of

these wild Caledonians. The clash and conflict and mental friction incident to the process of Christianising these savage tribes must, from the nature of the case, have rendered the work a tedious one. Even with all our modern appliances and Christian organisations, how slowly is the work of converting the heathen carried on; how comparatively meagre are the results of Missions to heathen lands! One method adopted by these early Celtic Missionaries was, to go direct to the reigning chief or kingling, preach the Gospel to him, and get him to interpose his authority for the conversion of his subjects. This, which might be described as the method of gravitation, proceeded on the principle that the head of the tribe being won, the influence would filter down through all grades of the people—the leaven, being inserted in the centre, would soon leaven "the whole lump." However crude, or even absurd, this notion may appear to us, we must remember that *individualism*, whether in politics or religion, in the state of society that then existed, was an unknown quantity. Besides, are we certain that something very like this does not operate in modern society—that habits, and manners, and modes of thought, do not naturally tend to follow the law of gravitation, and descend from the upper to the lower grades of the social system? Another method of meeting the difficulty consisted in a system of compromise which has a curious illustration in the instructions given by Gregory the Great to Augustine, as recorded by Bede. According to this method the Christian

saint had to be substituted for the Pagan deity; the
holy day of the Church for the Pagan festival, and the
Pagan Temple converted into the Christian Church.
The Roman Basilica, or Judgment Hall, however, was
the model almost universally adopted for Christian
architecture. No doubt this policy was liable to great
abuse. It is, of course, true that all religions, as such,
must necessarily have a good deal in common; and it
would be an objection to any new religion, not a recommendation, that it was wholly unlike all that had
been known before. The question may, however, be
asked, whether this compromising policy was not
carried too far in the Mediæval Church, and whether,
to quote Fuller, "This new wine, put into old vessels,
did in after ages taste of the cask!" But undoubtedly
the principle was recognised in the early Church, when
the Jewish Passover merged in the Feast of the Resurrection, and Christmas took the place of the Pagan
Saturnalia and Solstitia. It had been exemplified by
our Lord in the adoption of the rite of baptism, for
which precedents might be cited both in Jewish and
other existing religious usages. The Church, however,
was more chary in the application of this principle
during the first ages, while Paganism, in its most idolatrous and licentious forms, was still a living power in
the world, though this caution perhaps increased the
difficulty of evangelising the rural populations of the
Empire, among which Paganism steadily survived for
centuries after Christianity was the authorised religion
of the State. The story of the professing convert who

continued to make his bow to the statue of Jupiter, in case his day should return, illustrates the same fact from another point of view. With this reservation, we may not minimise the force of Fuller's thunder, when he says: "In process of time, Christianity, keeping a correspondency and some proportion with Paganism, got a smack of heathen ceremonies." And in reference to the Pantheon, or "shrine of all gods" in Rome, which was turned into a Christian Church, he adds—"Surely they had better have built new nests for the holy dove, and not have lodged it where screech-owls and unclean birds had formerly been harboured. If the High Priest among the Jews was forbidden to marry a widow or a divorced woman, but that he should take a virgin of his own people to wife, how unseemly was it that God Himself should have the reversion of profaneness assigned to His service, and His worship wedded to the *relict*, yea (what was worse) *whorish* shrines, formerly abused with idolatry." By whatever method it was accomplished, we see the great work going on in our land, whereby in the sixth and seventh centuries barbarism is being baptised and made a new creature, the angel is being born, and the ape and tiger in us doomed. The wild Caledonian has caught a higher vision that will poison all meaner life for evermore. From the dim life of the past, with all its savage fierceness and absence of the feelings of true humanity, he was waking up to the contact of a supreme love, a motive that gave a sublime rhythm to life, a high initiation in the sphere of influences that modify and ennoble the being. Here, then, is a great landmark in the history of Christianity in our land. Here let the light of history shine forth, is the fond aspiration that involuntarily arises in our breast. But, alas, vain is the thought! For just here, where it would be so interesting to watch the spiritual transformation going on in our land, history limps. Our guides withdraw. The light grows less. Even with Bede we come into the stifling atmosphere of legend and myth, and after him silence and darkness reign. In vain do we long for the braced soul and hardy courage of the historical critic, who, "having climbed the lofty peaks of bygone centuries," has watched and noted the inevitable discovery and defeat of lies, the grandeur and beauty of truth. But already we know that the influence of Iona was beginning to be felt both in the north and south. There were religious establishments at Abernethy, Deer, and elsewhere, which, established by her monks, so grew in reputation that they began to rival the parent monastery. The Orkney Isles in the north, and Northumberland in the south, became the scene of missionary labours carried on by the brethren. From the wave-washed island of the Atlantic there thus streamed influences that filled our land and overflowed her boundaries, causing "the wilderness and the solitary place to be glad for them, and the desert to rejoice and blossom as the rose."

CHAPTER XI.

IT was at the close of the sixth century that Gregory I., Bishop of Rome, conceived the idea of
converting the Anglo-Saxons of Britain. In an
early age, as we have seen, Christianity was introduced into Britain. But the Celtic Church had well-
nigh perished under the influence of the heathen
invasion. The early Britons of the South had been
born to Christ, but needed to be born again! The
lamp of Divine truth had been succeeded by the
choke-damp of Saxon idolatry. Like a palimpsest
originally inscribed with the Gospel, and subsequently
written over with monkish legend and superstition,
the early features of Celtic Christianity that characterised South Britain were well-nigh lost in the
superincumbent heathenism with which they were
overlaid. Henceforth Christianity in the South par-
took, more or less, of the Roman form, while in the
north it existed for centuries in its insular Celtic
character. In the seventh century, what we now call
England, we see subject to a twofold spiritual invasion. Rome attacks it on the south, and Iona invades
it on the north. A consideration of this interesting

episode in the development of Christianity in Britain
will lead us out of our special field into the great,
broad highway of general history, in which we see
European society in a state of dissolution, and Christianity partaking of the general decay, called suddenly
to face wild hordes of Arabs, "earnest as death and
life," in the belief and propagation of a great truth and
a great lie—the great truth, "God is One"; the great
lie, "Mohammed is His prophet!" In this century,
then, while we see the Celtic Church in Scotland
rising into prominence, establishing monasteries everywhere throughout the land, sending out its Christian
and civilising influences in all directions, bulging over
into England, and even extending its missionary operations to the Continent, the outlook on the Continent
of Europe also presents a scene of more than usual
interest, in which learning and piety are beheld in a
state of decline. The natural simplicity which characterised the writings of the Apostolic age was now
succeeded by the coarse and confused jargon of the
schools. The lustre of the Gospel was eclipsed by a
cloud of corrupt opinions. Abuses crept in one by
one, and each paved the way for others, until an unseemly fabric of superstitious ceremony gradually
arose upon the ruins of genuine piety. An extravagant veneration for departed saints and martyrs, the
idolatrous worship of images and relics, the pride and
ambition of ecclesiastics, and, especially the low moral
tone of society, and the vices and follies of the people,
mark this as an age of melancholy decline. In this

state of things two striking figures emerge on the page of history—Mohammed and Gregory the Great. Each in his own way impressed his mark on that and succeeding ages. It may, perhaps, be thought a little out of place in a sketch of Scottish Church History to take into our view so wide a range ; but as we can only adequately understand our subject when seen in connection with the general development of Christianity, and the larger movements of the world ; and as Gregory is the man to whom we are, most of all, indebted for bringing Anglo-Saxon England into connection with Roman Christianity, he is deserving of notice here, as indicating the point of junction between Rome and South Britain, and as affording, as we shall afterwards see, some means of determining the complexion of our Celtic form of Christianity as distinguished from that of Rome. As to the other great figure, Mohammed, his only place here is as the embodiment of a great religious and military power outside of, and antagonistic to, Christianity, a force which, beginning in the deserts of Arabia, as a protest against idolatry, gradually assumed the dimensions of a power that threatened Christianity, and even civilisation itself. In Mecca, near the well which Hagar found with her little Ishmael, Mohammed was born (570 A.D.). To the Arab people this descendant of Ishmael was as a birth from darkness to light. To this obscure people, roaming unnoticed in the desert from the time of Abraham their father, a prophet appears, and the unnoticed becomes world-notable, the small

has grown world-great. Within one century afterwards Arabia is at Grenada on this hand, at Delhi on
that; glancing in valour, and splendour, and the light
of genius, Arabia shines through long ages over a
great section of the world. "These Arabs," says
Carlyle, "the man Mohammed, and that one century,
—is it not as if a spark had fallen, one spark, on a
world of what seemed black, unnoticeable sand; but
lo, the sand proves explosive powder, blazes heaven-
high from Delhi to Grenada." Extending our outlook,
then, beyond the European barrier, our attention is
arrested by the rise, in Asia, of a new power, in the
form of a hostile creed and a destroying enemy—a
power that not only threatened the national exist-
ences of Europe, but the Christian faith. It was in
the year 621 A.D. that Mohammed made his triumphant entry into Medina, in Arabia. At this point a
new stream of events begins to flow in the world's
history. This entry is called the Hegira, or Flight,
and forms the commencement of the Moslem chrono-
logy. At this place began that new form of religion
which is known by the name of its founder. The
worshippers were summoned by a voice sounding from
the highest pinnacle of the Mosque or Church, and
announcing the words which to this hour are heard
from every minaret in the East—"God is great! God
is great! There is no God but God. Mohammed is
the apostle of God. Come to prayers; come to
prayers. Prayer is better than sleep; prayer is better
than sleep." This new swarm from the desert soon

became the terror of Europe, They were not like the Goths or Huns—savage warriors to be turned aside with a bribe, or won by a prayer, but enthusiastic in what they considered a holy cause, flushed with victory, armed and disciplined in a style superior to anything the West could show. Ali, who married the favourite daughter of the chief, we are told "fought and prayed with the same irresistible force," and conquered the unbelievers with might and main, "cleaving armed men from the crown to the chin with one blow." Blow after blow resounded from these fierce warriors, till the majestic empires of the Greeks and Persians were laid low. And still the great march went on, and everywhere high-peaked mosques arose where formerly the basilicas of Christian worship stood. This was the initial encounter of the Crescent and the Cross, the struggle between Mohammedanism and Christianity, which culminated in the Crusades. Not altogether indiscriminate was the wrath of the Caliphs, as the successors of the prophet were called, against the professors of Christianity, as the following instructions from one of their number to the leaders of the host will show :—"Be just, and spare the feelings of the vanquished. Respect all religious persons who live in hermitages or convents, and spare their edifices. But should you meet with a class of unbelievers of a different kind, who go about with shaven crown, and belong to the synagogue of Satan, be sure you cleave their skulls, unless they embrace the true faith or render tribute." The monks were alarmed, and the monasteries were filled with exaggerated reports of the progress of this vast invasion. In their apparently sheltered positions, they could never be sure for an hour that the missionaries of the new faith would not be climbing over their walls with shouts of conquest, and giving them the option of conversion or death. The attitude of this power to ancient civilisation comes out with tragic hopelessness in the Christian legend of the destruction of the Alexandrian library, which contained a collection of MSS. so vast and valuable that it had no equal on earth. Said Omar the Caliph, to the general who was his informant as to the literary wealth it contained : " Either what those books contain is in the Koran, or it is not. If it is, these volumes are useless ; if it is not, they are wicked. Burn them." And so these records, of priceless worth—irrecoverable monuments of the past —were used to heat the baths of the city for many months—an everlasting disgrace to the Saracen name.

This apparently retrograde movement, however, in which the world was in danger of losing all the results of civilisation and all the lessons of Providence. represents rather the eddying of the stream, than a backward impulse. But to those contemporaries who were competent to take a large view of events from their standpoint, there was much in the aspect of things to cause not a little anxiety. The rapid advance of this alien power from the desert seemed like the sounding of the trump of doom over the old order of things, or letting the windlass run down after men had been turning at it painfully for generations. When Pope Gregory the Great first conceived the idea of sending Christian missionaries to evangelise Great Britain, the scheme and empire of the Prophet of Islam—that Empire which, before many years elapsed, extended from India to Spain—existed only in his mind. There it was fostered by study and meditation; and, moulded by a high poetical temperament, gave rise to visions and dreams which startled the repose of the world as a nightmare. Meanwhile Gregory, fired with Christian zeal, cherished the noble design of sending Christian missionaries to convert the heathen in various parts, and especially the Anglo-Saxons of Great Britain. Thus, unconsciously to each other, the two great powers of Christianity and Mohammedanism were being prepared for the impending struggle. The story of Gregory's celebrated mission for the conversion of this country is well known. It refers to the time before he sat in St. Peter's chair, while he was Abbot of the Monastery of St. Andrew's, Rome. Passing through the market-place of that city, on one occasion, he beheld exposed for sale several fair and beautiful children, with ruddy cheeks and blue eyes, and their fine yellow tresses flowing in long curls upon their shoulders. Inquiring from what country or nation they were brought, he was told from the island of Britain, whose inhabitants were of such personal appearance. Again inquiring, whether these islanders were Christians, or still involved in the errors of Paganism, and being informed

that they were Pagans, he sighed deeply, and said—
"Alas! what pity that the author of darkness is
possessed of men of such fair countenances; and that
being remarkable for such graceful aspects, their
minds should be void of inward grace." Again, therefore, he asked what was the name of that nation?
and, being answered that they were Angles, "Right,"
said he, "for they have an angelic face, and it becomes such to be co-heirs with the angels in heaven.
What is the name," proceeded he, "of the province
from which they are brought?" It was replied that
the natives of that province were called Deiri. "Truly
they are *De ira*," said he, "withdrawn from wrath,
and called to the mercy of Christ. How is the king
of that province called?" They told him his name
was Ælla; and he, alluding to the name, said, "Hallelujah, the praise of God the Creator must be sung in
those parts." This conversation may appear trifling,
but it was destined to produce the most important
results. St. Gregory immediately resolved on under-
taking a mission to Britain, with the permission of
Benedict I., the reigning Pope, and had even set forth
on his journey, in company with several monks of his
own monastery, when so great a clamour was raised
by the Roman people at the loss of so good a man,
that the Pope compelled his return. The idea, however, continued to occupy his mind; and when,
afterwards, he was elevated to the bishopric of
that see, he looked about him for a man of zeal
resolution, and piety, that might undertake the

mission, and such a one he found in Augustine the Monk.

It was on July 23, 596, that Gregory despatched Augustine on his mission to England, accompanied by thirty companions; and they set out with joy upon an expedition, of which the prize was to be either the conquest of a new nation to Christ, or the crown of martyrdom for themselves. Having passed through France, the missionaries embarked at Ebbsfeet, in the Isle of Thanet, whence they sent messengers to Ethelbert, king of Kent, to inform him that they were come from Rome, and soliciting an interview. Ethelbert, whose queen Bertha was a Christian, appointed Augustine a day when he and his companions should appear before him. At the time appointed Augustine and his companions proceeded to the royal presence, where seats had been prepared for them. At the command of the king, they preached to him and his nobles the Word of life. "They told," says an old Saxon author, "how the mild-hearted Healer of mankind, by His own throes of suffering, set free this guilty middle-earth, and opened to believing men the door of heaven." Ethelbert's answer, as given by Bede, was both manly and sensible, and would not have disgraced the most enlightened philosopher—"Your words and promises are very fair, but as they are new to us, and of uncertain import, I cannot forsake the established customs of my nation. But because you have come from far into my kingdom; and, as I conceive, are desirous to impart to us those things which you believe to be true, and most beneficial, we will not molest you, but give you favourable entertainment, and take care to supply you with your necessary sustenance; nor do we forbid you by preaching to gain as many as you can to your religion." This favourable response filled them with joy. The final conversion of Ethelbert speedily followed, who sought, at the hands of the missionaries, the sacrament of baptism; and his long reflection and deliberation on the subject afforded good hope of his sincerity. The Queen, already a zealous missionary, and the king being secured, the Gospel triumphed in the realm. Within a short period the inhabitants of Kent were convinced of their folly in worshipping Thor and Woden, the gods of their ancestors, and so earnestly did they listen to Augustine, that thousands were baptised, and made open profession of Christianity.

That the way was prepared in Saxon England for the reception of the Gospel even before the mission of Augustine, is evident from the Epistles of Gregory, who asserts that the Saxons were not only desirous to receive the Christian faith, but had also signified their desire to the clergy of France, whom he blames for their refusal "to assist them in their good motions and encourage their piety." This pious inclination in the Saxons, in all probability, proceeded from the influence and example of the British Christians who resided among them—and the fact itself had probably come to the knowledge of Gregory through the Queen. While this movement was going on in the south, another was set on foot in the north. Christianity had entered Saxon England at its two extremities. Augustine and his monks beginning in Kent, had extended their teaching and influence over the south and south-west of the kingdom, while Aidan and his monks had entered Northumberland, and pushed their teaching and influence over the northern, and eastern, and midland provinces. Thus Rome and Iona met on English ground, and Italian and Celtic missionaries contended for the mastery. Between them England suffered a spiritual conquest, threw away her idols, abandoned Thor and Woden, and embraced Christianity. The first Celtic missionary who went from Iona to Northumberland was a man of an austere disposition, who could make no impression upon the people. He returned with the story of his failure, and reported that the Northumbrians were people of "a stubborn and barbarous disposition," whom it was hopeless to think of converting to Christianity. An aged monk, on hearing the doleful tale of failure, rose up, when the matter was debated in the monastery, and addressing himself to the weak brother who had abandoned the mission field, said— " I am of opinion, brother, that you were more severe to your unlearned hearers than you ought to have been, and did not at first, conformably to the Apostolic rule, give them the milk of more easy doctrine, till being by degrees nourished with the Word of God, they should be capable of greater perfection, and be able to practice God's sublimer precepts." That speech pointed out the speaker as the fittest man to deal with the barbarous Saxons, and Aidan (for he it was who thus spoke) was ordained by the Presbyter Monks of Iona.   And though he was now a man of nearly eighty years of age, he undertook the mission with cheerfulness and alacrity, and at once set his face towards Northumberland.

CHAPTER XII.

THE missionary zeal which was kept alive by a
succession of learned and pious Abbots in the
Monastery of Iona went forth in all directions,
till the whole of Scotland was evangelised. Nor did
the labours of the monks stop here. But, as Alexander, after he had conquered the world, expressed
the wish that there were more world's to conquer, so
these missionaries, fired with zeal, could not be re-
strained within the limits of their own country, but
carried the light of Christianity to England and the
Continent. As we have already seen, the Anglo-
Saxons of England attracted the notice of Gregory
of Rome who sent missionaries to convert them from
their idols to Christianity. A little later the Culdees
issued from their headquarters in Iona on the same
great enterprise. These two streams of Christian
propagandism met on English ground. The Roman
missionaries advanced from the South, while the
Scottish evangelists issued from the North. The
carcase—England with its Anglo-Saxon idolatry—

was attacked on the south by the Roman eagles, on
the north by the Scottish lion. Between the two
forces, the spiritual conquest of England was a fore-
gone conclusion.

We have already seen how Ethelbert, king of Kent,
was converted to Christianity through the labours of
Augustine. It will be both interesting and instructive to note some typical examples of the progress
made by these missionaries, Roman and Scottish, in
the conversion of the Anglo-Saxons of Britain. Edwin,
king of Northumberland, who reigned in the third
decade of the century, seemed to have been more
powerful than any of his predecessors, being monarch
of all England, a circumstance which, as Bede observes,
was "*in auspicium suscipiendæ fidei*,"—"a favourable omen for the faith" he was afterwards to receive.
"God first made him great and after gracious," says
Fuller, "that so, by his power, he might be the more
effectual instrument of His glory." Meanwhile he had
married *Edelberga*, daughter of Ethelbert, king of
Kent, and was thus brought within the influence of
the missionaries of the south. The story of his
espousals is not without interest. Having sent ambassadors to ask her in marriage of her brother Ead-
bald, who then reigned in Kent, that king demurred,
on the ground that "It was not lawful to marry a
Christian virgin to a Pagan husband." But a compromise was effected. Edwin promised to observe an
attitude of strict neutrality towards the Christians,
giving his queen, and all her attendants, priests, or

ministers, perfect religious freedom. He also further promised that he himself would embrace the Christian religion if, " being examined by wise persons, it should be found more holy and more worthy of God." Whereupon the virgin was sent to Edwin, and Paulinus, a Roman missionary, a "man beloved of God," was ordained Bishop to go with her, and by daily exhortations, and "celebrating the heavenly mysteries, to confirm her and her company, lest they should be corrupted by the company of the Pagans." But the king was obstinate—proof against the tender solicitations of his queen, and as for the earnest appeals of the missionaries, he glided through them unstruck for a long time, "buoyant and evasive as a bee amongst hailstones." But serious thought at length came to him. An envenomed dagger, sent from the king of the West Saxons, was thrust at him, when one of his guard interposed, and received it, and fell dead, loyalty's martyr, at his feet. This produced a powerful impression on him. He became partly convinced of the truth of the Christian religion, and often debated the matter with his own thoughts as well as with others. And yet, quaintly observes Fuller, "he durst not entertain truth, a lawful king, for fear to displease custom, a cruel tyrant." Among the many debates he had with his counsellors on this subject, two passages from Bede may here be cited (book 2, cap. 13). The first is what purports to be a speech spoken by Coify, the prime Pagan priest, at a council of Edwin's nobles, held A.D. 627. "Surely," says he,

" these gods whom we worship, are not of any power or efficacy in themselves; for none has served them more conscientiously than myself; yet other men, less meriting of them, have received more and greater favours from their hand, and prosper better in all things they undertake. Now, if these were gods of any activity, they would have been more beneficial to me, who have been so observant of them." The logic of this Pagan priest limps, no doubt, but, as Fuller well observes, "let none wonder, if the first glimmering of grace in Pagans be scarce a degree above blindness." But the king was too astute a man to be thus caught. Though shivering on the brink of the change from Saxon idolatry to Christianity, he could not, all at once, launch out on the deep, with nothing but such air-bags, so suddenly blown out by Coify, to float his belief. Paulinus tried to get at him by direct Christian teaching, and in this was ably seconded by one of the chief men of the court, whose beautiful discourse, though dressed in a style more familiar than ornate, I quote from Bede (book 2, cap. 13)—"The present life of man, O king, seems to me, in comparison of that time which is unknown to us, like to the swift flight of a sparrow through the room wherein you sit at supper in winter with your commanders and ministers, and a good fire in the midst, whilst the storms of rain and snow prevail abroad; the sparrow, I say, flying in at one door and immediately out at another, whilst he is within is safe from the wintry storms, but after a short space of fair weather he immediately vanishes out of your sight into the dark winter from which he had emerged. So this life of man appears for a short space, but of what went before, or what is to follow, we are utterly ignorant. If, therefore, this new doctrine of Christianity contains something more certain, it seems justly to deserve to be followed." At that council others spoke to the same effect. Paulinus preached. The Pagan priest was converted, confessed the utter hollowness of Paganism, advised the king to "instantly abjure and set fire to those temples and altars" which had been consecrated by them "without reaping any benefit from them." The king consented, when, suiting the action to the word, Coify, having girt a sword about him, with a spear in his hand, mounted the king's stallion, and proceeded to the temple, which he destroyed, with all its idols and enclosures, by fire. The name of the place where this occurred is called Godmanham (in Bede's time *Good-mundingham*, or "the home of the protection of the gods"), and is situated in the East Riding of Yorkshire, not far from the city of York. Here Paulinus built the parish church, wherein is the font in which he baptised the heathen priest Coify. At length, after much doubt and deliberation, Edwin the king formally embraced Christianity, and he and his nobles received the sacrament of baptism on Easter day, being the 12th of April, A.D., 627, in a church which he himself had built in York during the time he was receiving instruction in the Christian faith. Thus the king was subdued to Christianity at last, and if his

disposition was typical of that of his subjects, it may
lead us to tone down our censure of Corman, the predecessor of Aidan, who, as we saw in our last lecture,
having gone from Iona to convert the Northumbrians,
soon gave up the task as hopeless, and returned to his
native monastery to report that nothing could be made
of them, as they were of a "stubborn and barbarous
disposition," for Edwin's heart was as a citadel be-
sieged yet strongly fortified on all sides. His action
in resisting so long the influence of Christianity may
serve to show, in a passing glance, the nature of the
struggle then going on between Heathenism and the
Gospel in Britain. The queen had used her private
influence with him. The Pope, Boniface, had written
to her reminding her of the words of St. Paul, "the
unbelieving husband is sanctified of the wife," etc.
This appeal to the queen on behalf of her husband
was reinforced by Boniface by the present which he
sent her of a silver looking-glass and a gilt ivory
comb. Once, we are told, when in exile, and in circumstances of danger in East Anglia, a vision had
appeared to him to offer him protection if he would
only change his religion by renouncing his idols and
becoming a Christian. If he believed in ghosts, as his
chronicler undoubtedly did, he was, it appears, not
over civil to the one referred to, for, according to the
narrative, as he stood beside the palace of his host,
Redwald, the king, at the dead hour of night, brooding
over the danger that he had been warned to fear from
his treachery, a strange apparition intruded on his

loneliness, and coming close up, saluted him, and asked him, "why he sat there alone and melancholy on a stone at that time when all others were taking their rest and were fast asleep?" Edwin replied in good Scotch fashion, "what was it to him whether he spent the night within doors or abroad?" It was, then, no easy task to gain over to Christianity this heathen king, but being won, he became a zealous missionary of the cross, and was instrumental, according to Bede, in persuading Eorpwald, king of the East Saxons, to "abandon his idolatrous superstitions, and with his whole province to receive the faith and sacraments of Christianity." Altogether Edwin was a man of strong conviction, and so inflexible was he in the administration of justice, that, as is attested by Bede, "in his days a woman with a babe at her breast might have travelled over the island without suffering an insult," and Paulinus, the instrument of the king's conversion, proved himself to be a willing and powerful ally, a great evangelist and pillar of the state. He was among those sent by Pope Gregory to Britain on hearing from Augustine that he had "a great harvest and but few labourers." His personal appearance is thus described by Bede on the authority of " a certain abbot of singular veracity:" "Tall of stature, a little stooping, his hair black, his visage meagre, his nose slender and aquiline, his aspect both venerable and majestic." And the power that accompanied his evangelistic labours laid prostrate that of the Saxon idolatry as Dagon was overcome by the ark of God. Many thousands of

Edwin's subjects were then converted and baptised by Paulinus in the river Swale, and shortly after we find him going north, and for six-and-thirty days together instructing the people of Bernicia, and baptising them in the river Glen.

The circumstances of Edwin's death are thus recorded. In 633 Cadwalla, king of the Britons, rebelled against him, being supported by Penda, a Pagan and a most warlike man. At Hatfield, in the West Riding of Yorkshire, about seven miles to the north-east of Doncaster, a great battle was fought in which Edwin was slain and his army routed. He was then forty-seven years of age, having reigned "most gloriously seventeen years over the nations of the English and the Britons," the six last years of his life as a Christian. After the battle, his head was brought to York, and deposited in the porch of St. Gregory, from whose disciples he had received the Word of life. The kingdom of the Northumbrians was then divided into two provinces, Deira and Bernicia, the former reaching from the Humber to the Tyne, the latter from the Tyne to the Tweed. Though not united into one community, the two states were generally governed by one monarch, and became at such times the most powerful of the Anglo-Saxon kingdoms. After the death of Edwin the kingdom was divided, Osric becoming king of the Deiri, and Eanfrid king of the Bernicians. Both of these men were Christians when they began to reign, but subsequently apostatised, and Cadwalla, the king of the Britons, through

whom they had mounted the throne, afterwards slew
them and reigned in their stead; and thus in Northumbria, as the result of tyranny and apostasy, the
Christians had at that period a bad time of it—men,
women, and children being alike the objects of savage
cruelty, and being "put to tormenting deaths." The
year that witnessed these untoward events, according
to Bede, "is looked upon as unhappy and hateful to
all good men, as well on account of the apostasy of
the English kings, who had renounced the faith, as of
the outrageous tyranny of the British king." Oswald,
next of the blood royal, and nephew to King Edwin,
succeeded to the throne of Northumbria. In his youth
Oswald became an exile in the mountains of Caledonia,
where he was brought up in the midst of Christian
influences. When he went to take possession of his
kingdom, then in the enemy's hand, he erected, at a
place called Denis's-brook, the sign of the holy cross,
and on his knees prayed to God that He would assist
His worshippers in their great distress. Victory was
his, and he sat on the throne. His first concern, now
that he had rest from his enemies, was that his nation
should receive the Christian faith. For, apparently,
the obstinacy of the former king, Edwin, in adhering
to Paganism, was characteristic also of his people, who
had never, as a whole, been evangelised, while the
interregnum of apostasy and persecution already
noticed had retarded the work so auspiciously begun
in that king's reign. Accordingly, Oswald sent to the
elders of the Scots, among whom himself and his

followers, when in banishment, had received the sacrament of baptism, " desiring they would send him a bishop, by whose instruction and ministry the English nation, which he governed, might be taught the advantages, and receive the sacraments of the Christian faith." It was in answer to this request that, as we saw in our last lecture, Aidan, "a man of singular meekness, piety, and moderation," was sent. On the arrival of Aidan the king appointed him his seat, as he desired, in the Isle of Lindisfarne. Beautifully situated on the Northumbrian coast, this isle commands a view of the town of Berwick on the north, from which it is separated by an arm of the sea about seven miles in breadth ; to the South Bamborough Castle is seen jutting out on a bold promontory. To the east stretches, far as the eye can reach, the open sea ; while, to the west, across a narrow channel, the shore exhibits a beautiful hanging landscape of cultivated country, graced with a multitude of hamlets, villages, and woodlands. This island, a second Iona, became a centre of missionary operations whence the Culdees carried the Gospel to the half of the English nation—the northern half, the Roman missionaries operating on the other or southern half from their seat in Canterbury. Aidan appears to have been a man of a most exemplary life, zealous in the cause of Christ, and charitable to the poor. He seldom travelled but on foot ; and, when invited to large feasts at court, used to arise after a short refection, and betake himself to his meditations. Many slaves he redeemed from captivity, making them first freemen, then Christians. The historian Bede has but one fault to find with him—he did not celebrate Easter at the time fixed by Rome. On this account he says of him that "he had a zeal of God, although not fully according to knowledge." Yet he faithfully records that he and his followers, in their devotion to the religious life; their continual contemplation; their reading of Scripture; and learning of the Psalter, were a contrast and standing rebuke to his own age. His words are—"*Tantum vita illius a nostri temporis segnitiâ distabat.*" "So much differed his life from the laziness of our age." In him the king had a man according to his own heart. The nation was well off, blessed with a pious king and a pious priest. There was one difficulty Aidan had to contend with. He knew not the English language spoken by the people, and the people understood not the Gaelic language which was his mother tongue. But this difficulty was solved by the king, who, knowing both languages, consented to act as interpreter to the people, giving the English rendering of the discourses of Aidan spoken in the Gaelic. It must indeed have been a goodly sight to see the two pious men—priest and king—going thus hand-in-hand in the work of con-verting the heathen. The saintly monk, austere in his own conduct, indulgent to others, we seem to see traversing town and country on foot, and inviting every passer by to embrace the faith. The pious king, also humbly and willingly giving ear to his admoni-

tions, we see building and extending the Church of
Christ in his kingdom; and we fully endorse the
sentiment of Bede when he says, quoting evidently
from some contemporary source: " It was most de-
delightful to see the king himself interpreting the
Word of God to his commanders and ministers." We
are not, therefore, surprised to learn that, in the language of Bede—"From that time many of the Scots
came daily into Britain, and with great devotion
preached the Word to those provinces of the English
over which King Oswald reigned, and those among
them that had received priest's orders administered
to them the grace of baptism. Churches were built
in several places; the people joyfully flocked together
to hear the Word; money and lands were given of
the king's bounty to build monasteries; the English,
great and small, were, by their Scottish masters, instructed in the rules and observance of regular discipline, for most of them that came to preach were
monks." Lately, on visiting one of the most beautiful
spots in the Highlands of Inverness-shire, where a
Benedictine monastery had been erected by some who
formerly were Protestants, but who have joined
the Romish communion, I was informed that the son
of a Wigtownshire laird, one of the inmates, regarding whom I made inquiries, took the name of Brother
Oswald. On asking one of the brethren, who showed
us through the monastery, whence the name was
derived, he said—" King Oswald." Though we may
not apply the epithet " pervert " to men so devoted as

those who have thus renounced Protestantism, put the new wine of the nineteenth century into the old bottles of mediævalism, and inserted a bit of the past into the present, yet we cannot help thinking that they have looked at the past through the wrong end of the telescope, and perpetrated the solecism, in this age, of a crab movement, in renouncing Protestant freedom to kiss the Pope's toe.

CHAPTER XIII.

TOWARDS the close of the seventh century an era of hopelessness had set in. Darkness that might be felt settled down on Europe. The star of human progress was at its nadir. The continent was a scene of divided peoples and worn-out kings; an indolent church, and exhausted fields. It was an age of despair—when manhood, patriotism, and Christianity were at the lowest ebb. It is difficult to discern in the picture the least ray of hope. Of course each particular age is entitled to be judged on its own merits. It may not seem to be in advance of its predecessor, or to be vitally connected with the progressive features of succeeding times, but to exist in a state of aloofness from both, and to exhibit some special features of its own. That is to some extent true of the age to which our inquiries have conducted us. It is an age in which the civil power is declining and the ecclesiastical power is growing in strength. The old empire is in ruins, and the débris has not yet been organised into life. And the age has come into existence burdened with an inheritance of evils from the past almost too great for it to cope with. The elements of social and political order are in a state of solution, and the time for their crystallisation in feudalistic moulds is not yet. The rise of the spirit of Popery, on the background of this chaos of civil power, meets us at every turn. At Antioch, and Constantinople, and Alexandria, unseemly disputes are carried on in regard to ecclesiastical power and primacy. The rise and progress of this spirit, which began to show itself even in Apostolic times (Luke xxii. 24), must be here dealt with in the briefest manner. Originally there were no diocesan bishops in the Church. The election of one of the Presbyters to preside over the others at their deliberations led to the innovation ; the office of president suggesting, when it was made perpetual, that of overseer or bishop. As early as the second century men began to value the bishop, or pastor of the church, according to the size of the city where he dwelt. As the city of Rome had gradually acquired dominion over the rest of the civilised world, the Bishops of Rome early began to assume supremacy over the Church. Imitating the gradations of power in the State, the Church soon had (1) the Bishop, overseer of his parish ; (2) the Metropolitan, overseer of the province ; (3) the Patriarch, overseer of the Metropolitans ; and (4) eventually the Pope, overseer of all. Finding one supreme head of the Roman empire, they aimed at making one supreme head of the Church. It seemed vain to seek this supreme ruler in the East. For there Constantinople, Alexandria, Antioch, and Jerusalem, formed a sort of balance of power. And when Constantinople began to get the upper hand in ecclesiastical affairs, the three other eastern churches applied to the Church of Rome for help. Though the foundation of the Pope's temporal power was not laid till the middle of the eighth century, his ecclesiastical power had been steadily growing for centuries. At the time when Gregory sent Augustine to convert the Anglo-Saxons of Britain, it was advancing with resistless sweep. Pope Gregory seemed to be unconscious of it, yet undoubtedly it was then in the air. And the very elements of character that determined the influence of this great and good man were powerfully contributing to this result, notwithstanding all his efforts to the contrary. What his views on the subject were may be gathered from his own extant epistles. At the end of the sixth century, when the seat of Empire had been removed to Constantinople, John, Bishop of that place, began to assume the title of universal bishop. The same title was claimed by Cyriacus, his successor in that see, which drew from Gregory an indignant protest. " Far, very far," he says, " be it from a Christian mind, that any person should wish to snatch to himself a title whence he may seem, even in any the smallest degree, to diminish the honour of his brethren. To consent to the adoption of that wicked appellation is nothing less than to apostatise from the faith." Again, he says, "I tell you confidently, that whosoever calls himself, or wishes to be called, Universal Priest, does, in his self-

exaltation, anticipate Antichrist, because, through his
pride he exalts himself above his fellows." In his
epistle to John of Constantinople, he had said that "the
bulk of the iniquity was weighty enough to sink and
destroy all. And therefore I am bold to say, that
whoever uses or affects the style of Universal Bishop,
has the pride and character of Antichrist." Again, in
his letter to Anastatius, Bishop of Antioch, he has
these words upon the same subject—"Cyriacus and
myself can never be made friends, and come to any
good understanding, unless he is willing to give up
the vanity and usurpation of his style. This is a
point of the last importance, neither can we comply
with the innovation, without betraying religion, and
adulterating the faith of the Catholic Church. For,
not to mention the invasion upon the honour of your
character, if any one bishop must have the title of
universal, if that Universal Prelate should happen to
miscarry, the whole Church must sink with him."
Thus far removed from Popish pretensions was the
man who may be viewed as the founder of the
Anglican Church, and no other vindication is needed
for the breaking of that Church from the see of Rome.
It is not the case of the man who kicks over the
ladder by which he has mounted; but of a great
community that severs itself from a system that has
developed in wrong lines. An appeal from mediævalism to antiquity is the ample justification, as it is
the very *raison d'être*, of the Anglican Church. It
might be imagined by the uncharitable that Gregory's

opposition to papal pretensions arose to some extent from the fact that others claimed that position, and that had he himself had that dignity conferred on him, his objections would have melted away. But this supposition is in direct opposition not only to the well-known character of Gregory, but to the facts of the case. In his letter to Eulogius, bishop of Alexandria, he complains loudly to that patriarch for saluting him with the title of Universal Bishop. "If your holiness," says Gregory, "treats me with the title of Universal Bishop, you exclude yourself from an equality of privilege. But, pray, let us have none of this. Let us not feed our vanity with pompous appellations; for this is the way to weaken the grace of charity, and disserve us in our best qualities." Thus, although the spirit of Popery seemed then to be in the air, Gregory did his best to exorcise it, and to keep himself aloof from it, which undoubtedly he, to a large extent, succeeded in doing; only, in a nature like his, a great deal goes on beneath the surface of consciousness, and determines the future, without the man himself being aware of it. The spirit of the age was too much for him. It was, unconsciously to himself, influencing him; he was, if not the creature of that age, at least an embodiment of it in some of its better aspects.

Such, briefly, was the stage of development to which the Church of Rome had attained when its missionaries met those of Iona on English ground. In the polity of the Empire it found a framework on which to model the constitution of the Church, which developed on these lines into a Holy Roman Empire, or City of God. The Celtic Church in Britain, on the other hand, was altogether simpler in its organisation and, far from the seat of empire, passed through no such development as that which culminated in the Roman Hierarchy. If the question be asked, was the organisation of the Celtic Church in Scotland Presbyterian or Episcopalian, the answer of an impartial judge must be that it was neither the one nor the other, but an order *sui generis*,—a system of Church polity which might develope into either, or even into something different from both. That there were persons bearing the name of bishops in very early times in Scotland is undoubted, but it is equally undoubted—(and on this subject I may be permitted to quote the words of the late Dean Stanley in his lectures on the History of the Church of Scotland)—that " they" (the bishops) " had no dioceses, no jurisdiction, no territorial Episcopal succession. Their orders were repudiated by the prelates of England and France in those ages. The Primate of the Church of Scotland, for the first 300 years of its history, was not a bishop, but a presbyter—first the Abbot of Iona, and then of Dunkeld. The succession, such as it was, was a succession, not of Episcopal hands, but of Columba's relics. Early bishops of St. Andrews, of Glasgow, and the like, figured in legends, but they had no existence in fact. The abbot, not the bishop, was regarded as the ordinary ecclesiastical ruler, and the superiors of the various monasteries, by which the country was evangelised, looked to the chief abbot, who sat in Columba's chair, as the head of their whole Church. This much," says the Dean, "is acknowledged by all." It seems a valid inference, too, from the narrative of Bede—and this also is allowed by the Dean, that Columba and his successors consecrated the bishops whom they sent forth to England. " They certainly," says he, "gave them their jurisdiction, and it was, therefore, not altogether unlikely that the Episcopal succession of the northern provinces of England had been deeply coloured by Presbyterian blood." It seems, on the whole, that the gap—ever widening in the Roman Church—between the presbyter and bishop, the monks of Iona were not aware of; or, if they knew the fact that peculiar honours and functions were now reserved for the one and denied to the other, it is plain they had determined to ignore it. It would be interesting, had we the necessary data, to compare the two forms of Christianity—the Roman and the Celtic—that thus divided Anglo-Saxon Britain between them in the seventh century. But the student of that period, while he finds himself, in either camp, walking in a familiar atmosphere, and breathing a healthy Christian air, cannot make out the landmarks of dogma. To those who seek for definite schools and forms of thought, this age and place will bring disappointment, it will be their despair. Certainly no Church then was more full of a true missionary spirit than that of Iona, and yet no Church was less explicit on particular doctrinal forms. It appears, indeed, from an epistle of Pope Honorius (625-638) written to the Scots, that the "poison of the Pelagian heresy" infected them. They are accordingly exhorted to put away from their thoughts "all such venomous and superstitious wickedness," and to remember that "that insolent and impious proposition, 'That man can live without sin of his own free will, and not through God's grace,' was condemned, and abolished these 200 years," and was "also daily anathematised for ever by us." But this same Pope, who was so zealous a defender of the doctrine of original sin, was more than suspected of being tainted with the heresy of the "Monothelites," whose views he undoubtedly encouraged. As Liberius, nearly two centuries before, was an Arian, Honorius was a Monothelite—rather hard nuts for the advocates of Papal infallibility to crack! But this by the way. There was a dash of Pelagianism in the doctrine of the Scots, and a taint of Monothelitism in that of the Pope. But possibly these elements were neutralised in the tide of missionary zeal that set in, or in the interaction of Celtic and Romanised forms of Christian thought. The truth is, that the differences then existing between the Roman and Celtic forms of Christianity were mainly confined to subsidiary matters, such as the time for the observance of Easter, and the form of tonsure. According to Usher, in his "Religion of the ancient Irish," the difference is thus explained. The Romans observed Easter between the 15th and

21st day of the moon, immediately after the 21st day
of March. In reckoning the age of the moon, they
followed the Alexandrian cycle of nineteen years, or
the Golden Number, as interpreted and explained by
Dionysius Exiguus. The Celts, on the other hand,
kept Easter on the Sunday that fell betwixt the 14th
and 20th day of the moon; and followed, in their
computation of it, not the nineteen years cycle of
Anatolius, but a cycle of eighty-four years attributed
to Sulpicius Verus. With regard to the tonsure, the
other subject in debate between the two contending
parties, the Roman clergy shaved the crown of the
head, which was surrounded by a circle of hair, supposed to represent the wreath of thorns forced by the
cruelty of his persecutors on the brow of the Messiah,
a custom which they declared to have been handed
down to them from St. Peter. The Celtic missionaries, on the other hand, permitted the hair to grow on
the back, and shaved the forepart, of the head, from
ear to ear, in the form of a crescent, which their
opponents called, in derision, the tonsure of Simon
Magus. This matter of the tonsure appears to have
originated among the earliest Christian ascetics, who
regarded it as a token of their renunciation of the
world; but afterwards it came to be looked upon as a
necessary mark of the priestly caste. Besides these
two forms of tonsure, the circular and semicircular, a
third was also in use in early times, called the Oriental
or St. Paul's tonsure, which consisted in shaving the
whole head. History does not enlighten us as to who

were the founders of these several tonsures; but, whoever they were, they deserve to be honourably mentioned by the corporation of the barbers! Augustine
tried to reason with the Celts, to get them to conform
in these matters to the Roman custom, but in vain.
Laurentius, his successor in Canterbury, wrote a letter
to "his most dear brothers the lords, bishops, and
abbots throughout all Scotland," stating that he had
expected they would have been better informed about
Easter than the Britons, but that he had discovered
his mistake, and he goes on to add that a certain
Scotch bishop, called Dagan, had carried matters so
high as to refuse to eat with him, or even to take his
repast in the same house where he and his friends
were entertained. "There is a stupidity, as has been
well said, "against which the gods themselves fight in
vain." And doubtless the Roman priests thought
their Celtic brethren sufficiently endowed with the
faculty of obstinacy, at least, from their persistent
refusal to give up reckoning time by an old and erro-
neous almanac, and their steady adherence to a heretical tonsure. To us, in these times, when the very
fundamentals of Christianity are sometimes beheld
set under the Damoclean sword of modern thought,
such controversies are apt to provoke a smile; and yet,
when we come to think of it, with all our culture and
breadth of view, there are questions which divide the
Churches of Christendom in our day which are not
much larger than those we are considering. For, not
to mention the minute questions, almost microscopical,

which divide Presbyterians, the strange sight is presented in our day of violent feuds among our Episcopalian brethren, over such things as the position or dress of a priest! I have read of a barber's shop being characterised as "the focus of Florentine intellect," and "the navel of the earth." What the barber was in these old controversies, the milliner or draper would seem to be in some modern feuds. This controversy at length reached a crisis. The time came when the question must be decided, and men left to live at peace either together or apart. The Synod of Whitby (A.D. 664) was the result. The good Aidan at Lindisfarne escaped the pressure of Rome in these matters. Not so Finan, his successor. Eanfleda, the Queen of Northumberland, had been brought up in Kent, and had brought with her a Kentish priest, Romanus by name, who followed the new or Roman style in the celebration of Easter, and thus it happened, awkwardly enough, in the palace, that when the king had ended the time of fasting, and kept his Easter, the queen and her followers were still fasting, and celebrating Palm Sunday. But Finan stood firm, defied the courtly influences, resisted the infection of Roman innovation, and died in the faith of Iona. It was left to his successor, Colman, also a Culdee, to witness the grand climax in this controversy. The place where this synod was held was the monastery of Streoneshalch, where the Abbess Hilda then presided, and which overlooked the German Ocean from the cliffs of Whitby. At this Synod the Roman view

was represented by Agilbert, bishop of the West
Saxons, with the priests Agatho and Wilfrid, James
and Romanus, while the views of Iona were represented by Bishop Colman and his Scottish clerks, the
Abbess Hilda, and Bishop Ced, who acted as interpreter throughout. The king, Oswy, who, along with
his son, Alfrid, was also present, opened the controversy, and attempted to pour oil on the troubled
waters. Colman declared that the view held in Iona
as to the time for the celebration of Easter, had de-
scended by tradition from John, the disciple beloved
of the Lord. Wilfred held that if John really taught
this he was wrong, and that St. Peter taught them
differently. Colman referred to the piety of Columba,
which had been attested by miracles. But Wilfrid
replied by scornfully suggesting the hope that Iona's
great Abbot might not at last be found among those
to whom, boasting that they had prophesied, and cast
out devils, and done wonderful works, our Lord would
say, "I never knew you." Columba could not, in any
case, be compared to the prince of the apostles, to
whom our Lord entrusted the keys of the kingdom of
heaven. And when Wilfrid had quoted the passage
in which our Lord, addressing Peter, says, " I will give
unto thee the keys of the kingdom of heaven," a profound impression seemed to have been produced on
the mind of the king, who said, "Is it true, Colman,
that these words were spoken to Peter by our Lord ? "
and when he replied " It is true, O king "; " Then,"
concluded the king, " I also say unto you that he is

the door-keeper whom I will not contradict, but will, as far as I know, and am able, in all things obey his decrees, lest, when I come to the gates of Heaven, there should be none to open them." This ended the debate, and victory was on the side of Rome.

CHAPTER XIV.

Conclusion—The Abbess Hilda—The Poet Cædmon—St. Cuthbert—The Venerable Bede.

IN bringing this series of these sketches to a close, I have to lay before you four portraits—the Abbess Hilda, the Poet Cædmon, St. Cuthbert, and the Venerable Bede—as characteristic illustrations of the intellectual and religious life in this country at the close of the seventh century. Bede, living half his life in the seventh, and the other half in the eighth century, will form an appropriate link to connect this with a future series. With him we say good-bye for the present. We have now reached the very darkest edge of that calamitous night that fell on Europe, introducing a dreary waste of years, empty of all noble intellectual and spiritual life. And before looking out into the darkness, the vision of something noble and true in our poor human nature will be as a delightful hovering fancy to relieve the impending gloom—a sort of Indian summer, whose glory will project its brightness into the desolation of winter.

THE ABBESS HILDA (614-680 A.D.)

In those dim ages where we find queens to be "nursing mothers to the Church," and the very salt of society, Hilda occupies a position of eminence. She appears as a woman in whom the love of the Saviour is the supreme fact of her existence—a motive that gives a sublime rhythm to her life. And as from the watch tower of her faith she, a Christian sentinel, is on the look-out in her Master's cause, we seem to be invited to contemplate one whose whole life is set to heavenly music. Hilda was a high-born noble lady, being the daughter of Hereric, nephew to King Edwin. Like that king, she had been converted from idolatry to Christianity through the preaching of Paulinus. In the troubles of the time that saw her birth, her father, who "lived in banishment under Cerdic, King of the Britons," was poisoned. Her mother, Pregusuit, had a strange dream that night. She fancied she was seeking for her husband most carefully, and could find no sign of him anywhere; but after having used all her industry to seek him, she found a most precious jewel under her garment, which, whilst she was looking on it very attentively, cast such a light as spread itself throughout all Britain. "This dream," says Bede, "was brought to pass in her daughter, whose life was a bright example, not only to herself, but to all who desired to live well." The incidents of her life are few and brief, but interesting and suggestive. Christianity took a deep hold of her convictions, and a life of absolute consecration to God was the result. And as the highest form of consecration, according to the spirit of the age, was the monastic life, she resolved to quit the secular and embrace the religious life by taking the vow and veil. This resolution being taken, she withdrew into the province of the East Angles (Norfolk and Suffolk), to the king of which she was related. Thence she wished to pass over to France, 'that, forsaking her native country and all she had, she might live a stranger for our Lord's sake. In the monastery of Chelles, ten miles from Paris, her sister Heresuid, mother to Ald-wulf, King of the East Angles, lived under regular discipline. Thither she intended to go; but, after remaining a whole year in East Anglia, Bishop Aidan introduced her to the monastic life in a retreat on the north side of the river Wear, where, for the next year, she, with a few companions, lived the life of consecration. After this she went to a monastery called Heruteu (Hartlepool), in which she was made abbess. This monastery had been founded, not long before, by a pious woman of the name of Heiu, the first woman, it seems, who in the province of Northumbria took upon her the habit and life of a nun. She, too, had been consecrated by Aidan, but had gone elsewhere (to Tadcaster), thus causing the vacancy which Hilda filled up. Here Hilda's fame for sanctity and learning blazed forth. Attracted by her piety, Aidan and other religious men frequently visited her, and learned men were drawn to her because of "her innate wisdom" and inclination to the service of God. Profiting by their instructions, she organised the monastery, "reducing all things to a regular" system. It was after she had for some years governed this establish-

K

ment that she set to work to build that monastery at Whitby (Streaneshalch), as abbess of which she is best known to fame. This establishment she soon made the home of regular discipline. Here were diligently cultivated, under her fostering care, the virtues of justice and chastity, and the graces of piety, peace, and charity. The study of Scripture, and the active Christian life to which the inmates were devoted, made it a training school out of which men proceeded fully equipped for ecclesiastical duties and the service of the altar. The names of five bishops—all men of singular merit and sanctity—have been handed down as proceeding from this house. Among the five are found the famous St. John of Beverley and Wilfrid of York. The others were Bosa of York; Hedda of Dorchester, then Winchester; and Oftfor of Worcester. This wonderful woman, whom all called "Mother," was perhaps the most influential of all her contemporaries, male or female. Her piety shines out with living power as a great factor in the advancement of Christianity among the Anglo-Saxons. Her wisdom, admired of all, was such that kings thought it not beneath them to take her into their counsels, to ask and receive her advice. Like Huldah, the prophetess, in Josiah's reign, she was indeed a mother in Israel, to whom men would resort on all matters of the highest concern. As a patron of learning, she holds a distinguished place in connection with the most ancient English poet whose name has been handed down to us from the dust of antiquity.

CÆDMON (680 A.D.).

The story of Cædmon, the father of English song, interwoven as it is with that of Hilda, is invested with much interest. He lived near the monastery of Whitby. The date of his birth is unknown. His inspiration as a poet, in its initial stage, has thus been described. It was a favourite custom among the Anglo-Saxons to meet together at festivities. On such occasions the harp was moved round, and each in his turn was expected to sing or chant some poem to the instrument. These lays, it seems, were often the extempore composition of the singer, the art of poetry being extensively cultivated among our Saxon forefathers. Cædmon appears to have been a failure in this department of extempore poesy, being unable either to compose or sing. And when, on these occasions, he saw the harp approach him, he was so ashamed that he rose from his seat and went home. On one of these occasions, when he had thus withdrawn from the festive beer party in disgrace, he went home and laid himself down, giving way to a feeling of vexation and despondency, and fell asleep. In his slumber a stranger appeared to him, and, addressing him by his name, said, " Cædmon, sing me something." Cædmon answered, " I know nothing to sing, or I should not have left the hall to come here so soon." " Nay," said the stranger, " but thou hast something to sing!" " What must I sing?" said Cædmon. " Sing the Creation," was the reply. Cædmon immediately began to sing verses "which he had never heard before," and which are given in Anglo-Saxon in some of the old manuscripts. In the morning when he awoke he was a new man, possessed of the divine afflatus, able to compose at will the most excellent poetry. Accordingly he presented himself before the reeve or bailiff of Whitby, and informed him of his miraculous gift of poetry, and the reeve took him to the Abbess Hilda. That lady, with a number of high and pious ecclesiastics, listened attentively to his story, and witnessed his performances. After this they read to him a short portion of Scripture in Anglo-Saxon, and he went home, and on his return next morning he repeated it in Anglo-Saxon verse, excelling in beauty everything they had heard before. Such a heaven-born poet was a prize not to be thrown away, and Cædmon yielded to Hilda's earnest solicitations, embraced the religious life, and entered her monastery. Here, we are told, he was continually occupied in repeating to himself what he heard, and, "like a clean animal, ruminating it, he turned it into most sweet verse." Hilda ordered him to convert into verse the whole of the sacred history, a task he willingly undertook and successfully carried out. It has been noted that in his account of the fall, and that of Milton in "Paradise Lost," there are strong points of resemblance, and it has been suggested accordingly that the great Puritan epic poet had to some extent "ploughed with the heifer" of the monk of Whitby. The following verses, in which Satan is described as reviving from his overthrow, and which are taken from Thorpe's edition of Cædmon, are so like to the corresponding passage in Milton that they might well be taken for the original note of which the echo is in "Paradise Lost":—

"Boiled within him his thought about his heart;
Hot was within him his dire punishment.
Then spake he words : This narrow place is most unlike
The other that we formerly knew, high in heaven's kingdom,
Which my master bestowed on me, though we it, for the All-
    powerful, may not possess.
We must cede our realm ; yet hath he not done rightly,
That he hath struck us down to the fiery abyss of the hot hell,
Bereft us of heaven's kingdom, hath decreed to people it with
    mankind.
That is to me of sorrow the greatest, that Adam,
Who was wrought of earth, shall possess my strong seat ;
That it shall be to him in delight, and we endure this torment,
    misery in this hell.
Oh ! had I the power of my hands * * then with this host
   I ——
But around me lie iron bonds ;
Presseth this cord of chain ; I am powerless !
Me have so hard the clasps of hell so firmly grasped !
Here is a vast fire above and underneath ;
Never did I see a loathlier landskape ;
The flame abateth not, hot over hell.
Me hath the clasping of these rings, this hard polished band,
Impeded in my course, debarred me from my way.
My feet are bound, my hands manacled ;
Of these hell doors are the ways obstructed ;
So that with aught I cannot from these limb-bonds escape.
About me lie huge gratings of hard iron, forged with heat,
With which me God hath fastened by the neck.
Thus perceive I that he knoweth my mind, and that he knew
    also,
The Lord of hosts, that should us through Adam evil befall,
About the realm of heaven, where I had power of my hands."

It was early in the seventh century that St. Cuthbert appeared, a man, who from his consecration to a holy life and the activity and zeal put forth by him as a Christian missionary, stamped his age as a worthy successor of that which witnessed the heroic labours of St. Columba and Kentigern. A high promontory, round which swept the waters of the Tweed, was then the seat of a small monastery, bearing the descriptive name of Muilros (Old Melrose). A shepherd boy of the neighbouring vale of the Leader had seen this primitive abode of religious zeal and self-denial. Attracted by the force of Christian unworldliness that thus met his view, his soul burned within him, and it was only a question of time and opportunity that determined his entrance on the religious life. Admitted to the monastic life, he soon distinguished himself by his ardent but mild piety and zeal for the conversion of the heathen, and in due time rose to be superior or prior of the establishment. In the pages of the venerable Bede, his historian and contemporary, St. Cuthbert appears surrounded with a saintly halo amid the darkness of the Strathclyde and Northumbrian kingdoms, shooting athwart the field of history as a meteor, now in Strathtay, now in Ripon, then at Melrose, and finally at Lindisfarne, where in 664 A.D. he became abbot. This holy man, we are told, excelled all his brethren in devotion. While at Melrose he received from Boisil, a "priest of great virtue and of prophetic spirit," both the knowledge of the Holy Scriptures, and example of good works." After the death of Boisil, Cuthbert was placed over that monastery, where he instructed many in regular life, " both by the authority of a master and the example of his own behaviour." Nor did he confine his labours to the monastery, but " endeavoured to convert the people round about, far and near, from the life of foolish custom, to the love of heavenly joys." To prosecute these missionary labours, when he departed out of his monastery, he would often stay a week, sometimes two or three, and sometimes a whole month, before he returned home, continuing among the mountains to allure " that rustic people," by his preaching and example, to heavenly employments. A visit which he paid to the Solway is perpetuated in the name of Kirkcudbright (*Kirk-Cuthbert*). Being transferred to the island of Lindisfarne, he gave himself so truly to the spirit of prayer and heavenly contemplation, that " he appeared to others more like an angel than a man." To attain to still greater heights in devotion, he raised a solitary cell of unhewn stones and turf for his own habitation in the smaller island of Farne, where at length he died on the 20th of March, 687. Before going to Farne he had said, " If it shall please the Divine goodness to grant me, that I may live in that place by the labour of my hands, I will willingly reside there ; but, if not, I will, by God's permission, very soon return to you." The place, we are told, was quite destitute of water, corn and trees ; and, being

infested by evil spirits, very ill suited for human
habitation; but we are not surprised to learn that, on
his arrival, it became "in all respects habitable, and
the wicked spirits withdrew"—in which the modern
reader of Bede can see an ideal commentary on the
industry and piety of the saint, who by the one causes
the "desert" to become a "fruitful field," and by the
other chases away heathen darkness by the exhibition
of Gospel light. It is curious to note that the asceticism which distinguished St. Cuthbert in life long
lingered round his tomb. Until the Reformation, no
woman was suffered to approach his shrine; the cross
of blue marble still remains in the Durham Cathedral
floor which marked the limits beyond which female
footsteps were forbidden to pass, under pain of instant
and signal punishment from the offended saint. A
ludicrous instance of the saint's traditional aversion to
the fair sex is mentioned by Brand. "The Queen of
Edward III. having followed the King to Durham,
was conducted by him through the gate of the Abbey
to the prior's lodgings, where, having supped and gone
to bed with her royal lord, she was soon disturbed by
one of the monks who readily intimated to the king
that 'St. Cuthbert by no means loved the company of
her sex.'" The Queen, upon this, got out of bed, and
having hastily dressed herself, went to the castle for
the remaining part of the night, asking pardon for the
crime she had inadvertently been guilty of against the
patron saint of their Church. Interesting as is the
life of St. Cuthbert, with all its setting of legend, he

has what may be called a posthumous history exceed-ing in interest that of his actual life—a history curious in this, that it exhibits a human being more important dead than alive. The first chapter of this posthumous history relates to a period eleven years after his death, when, his brother monks, raising his body, that it might be placed in a conspicuous situation, found it uncorrupted and perfect. This they accepted as a miraculous proof of his saintly character. One hundred and seventy-four years afterwards, on the Danes invading Northumberland, the monks carried away the body of the saint, and for many years wandered with it from place to place throughout Northumbria and the south of Scotland, everywhere willingly supported by the devout, and this constitutes the second chapter of this strange history. Early in the eleventh century the saint's body was settled at the spot where afterwards in consequence arose the beautiful Cathedral of Durham. Here the saint was allowed to rest, after his posthumous pilgrimage, for five centuries, in which the shrine over the incorrupt body was enriched by the offerings of the faithful, till it became "a blaze of gold and jewellery, dazzling to look upon." In 1104 the body was inspected, and found still fresh, and again in 1540 it was examined with the same result. But in May 1827, or 1139 years after his death, the body was finally examined, and this time more rigorously than before, when it was found a mere skeleton, swaddled up so as to appear entire, with plaster balls in the eye sockets to

plump out that part of the visage. Thus a pious
fraud had established for itself a secure foundation in
the credulity of men for more than a thousand years.
The shock produced on the minds of those whose
pious superstition is thus suddenly emptied of its
reality, is like the dread of the pilgrim who has it
whispered to him that the holy places are a delusion.
It comes like the terror of the earthquake which
shakes the "sure and firm-set earth," when everything which we have regarded as solid and secure
trembles and gives way. But no such crisis of faith
comes to the man who reads in the pious legend the
transmitted impulse of one whose influence overflowed
his generation, and flowed down through the ages to
our own time. Such a one is proof against the shock,
as he has seen behind the legend; and from the backward swing of the pendulum, with all its devastating
force, his faith escapes, as fixed on that which is independent of myth and legend—as the mountain summit,
which, though swathed in mist, is yet there when the
cloud is scattered by the rising sun. Thus when we
pierce the film, and watch wreath after wreath of the
mists of legend in which tradition had invested him
pass away, with all the marvels of that wonderland in
which the devout imagination found a home for him,
St. Cuthbert stands out in this seventh century a leading embodiment of the saintly character; an influence
at once attractive and far-reaching; an example of
one whose exhibition in his own life of the Saviour's
compassion " makes a way where there was none be-

fore" into the hearts of men, and shakes dull souls till they start up and prophesy.

BEDE (673-735 A.D.).

A few words regarding the venerable Bede will form an appropriate sequel to this series of sketches. In the Abbess Hilda, the poet Cædmon, the saintly Cuthbert, and the venerable Bede, we have a quaternion of noble lives—lives which mirror the age—the latter half of the seventh century—in its best characteristics. But in Bede we have a "great teacher of religion, literature, and science." Latest of the three in entering the stage of life, he was perhaps the most illustrious man of his time. The place of his birth was in the territory afterwards belonging to the twin monasteries of St. Peter and St. Paul, at Wearmouth and Jarrow. It was in the third year of Egfrid, son of Oswy, the first of the kings of Northumberland after the union of the provinces Deira and Bernicia into one monarchy. The dominions of this king extended from the Humber to the Frith of Forth, and comprehended all the six northern counties of England, and the whole of the southern part of Scotland. In the Abbey of Wearmouth, at the age of seven years, he was placed under the care of the celebrated Abbot Benedict Biscop, and when the establishment of Jarrow, on the banks of the Tyne, was founded (A.D. 682), he appears to have gone thither under Ceolfrid, its first abbot, where he resided all the remainder of his life. These two monasteries, though five miles apart, from the unity and concord which prevailed between them, deserved rather, as Bede expresses it, to be called "one single monastery built in two different places." They were ruled for many years by Benedict himself, and his associates, Ceolfrid, Easterwin, and Sigfrid, a triumvirate of piety and peace. Bede was a youth of much talent, which he improved by studious habits and indefatigable industry. His thirst for knowledge had the most ample resources for its gratification in a library attached to the monasteries by Benedict Biscop. This man, a nobleman by birth, was unwearied in the pursuit of knowledge. He was a great traveller in many lands; and wherever he went he endeavoured to procure the most valuable books, and costly relics, and works of art, which could be had for money. Thus collected by him in the monasteries of Wearmouth and Jarrow, there was a library superior to any other in Britain, replenished with everything that could foster and develope a taste for learning. In such circumstances, Bede advanced in learning with such rapid strides, that although it was not usual to ordain deacons before they reached the age of twenty-five, he was promoted to that office at the early age of nineteen. His ordination was conducted by the celebrated John of Beverley, "at the bidding of Abbot Ceolfrid," as Bede himself relates. Such was his ardour in the pursuits of learning that, on the office of abbot being offered him, he declined the dignity on the express ground that it would curtail his leisure for study. "The office," as he expressed it, "demands thoughtfulness, and thoughtfulness brings with it distraction of the mind, which impedes the pursuit of learning." The peaceful tenor of his monastic life was apparently uninterrupted by absence or travel. His time was occupied in doing good, preaching the gospel, and with high consecration, fulfilling all the functions of the religious life he had embraced. He seldom or never moved beyond the limits of his own monastery, and yet, from its dark cloister, he surveyed the whole world, dispensing to men the gifts entrusted to him. He applied himself to every branch of literature and science then known; and "besides study, and writing comments on the Scriptures, he treated on several subjects—on history, astrology, orthography, rhetoric, and poetry." The names of his literary friends include Cuthbert, afterwards Abbot of Jarrow, to whom he inscribed his "Art of Poetry;" Eusebius, or Huetbert, to whom he inscribed his "*De Ratione Temporum,*" and his "Interpretation on the Apocalypse;" Constantine, to whom he inscribed his book "*De Divisione Numerorum;*" and Nothelm, then priest at London, and afterwards Archbishop of Canterbury, to whom he wrote his "Questions on the Books of Kings," etc. As Cædmon was happy in the patronage of the Abbess Hilda, so Bede was fortunate in the friendship of Ceolwulf, king of the Northumbrians, in one of whose provinces—Bernicia—he lived. The king, himself a man of singular learning, and a very great encourager of it in others, seems to have suggested to

Bede the writing of that work on which his fame principally rests—the "Ecclesiastical History," the papers of which our author submitted to his royal patron for perusal. It is perhaps to some extent due to the influence that Bede acquired over his royal patron and admirer that, as we read in the Saxon Chronicle, about three years after Bede's death, Ceol-wulf resigned his crown, and became a monk at Lindisfarne. In his last illness he was attended by Cuthbert, who had been one of his pupils, and after-wards became abbot of the monastery. From an early period of his life he seems to have been subject to a complaint which William of Malmesbury thus characterises: "He suffered in his stomach and drew his breath with pains and sighs." The Christian piety with which he suffered before his death has been the universal theme of panegyric. The whole scene of his increasing malady, his devout resignation, and fervent prayers for all his friends, together with his paternal admonitions for the regulation of their lives, and his uncontrollable anxiety to dictate to the boy who was his amanuensis, even to his last moments, are beautifully recorded in a letter written by Cuth bert. In that letter it appears "He was much troubled with shortness of breath, yet without pain;" and, towards the close, he passed his life, "cheerful and rejoicing, giving thanks to Almighty God, every day and night, nay, every hour, till the day of our Lord's ascension," 26th May, 735,—his last on earth. In his last days he was engaged translating the gospel of St.

John. "Go on quickly," he said to his amanuensis to whom he was dictating—"I know not how long I shall hold out." On the morning of his last day on earth, having spent the previous night in thanksgiving, one of his disciples said to him—"My dear master, there is still one chapter wanting; do you think it troublesome to be asked any more questions?" His answer was—"It is no trouble. Take your pen and make ready, and write fast." In the afternoon he summoned the brethren of the monastery on whom he bestowed "the gifts which God had bestowed" on him. The scene was affecting. They all mourned and wept, especially because he said "they should no more see his face in this world." "It is time," said he, "that I return to Him who formed me out of nothing. I have lived long. My merciful judge well foresaw my life for me. The time of my dissolution draws nigh, for I desire to die and to be with Christ." Having said much more, he passed the day joyfully till the evening, when his amanuensis said—"Dear master, there is yet one sentence not written." He replied, "It is well, you have said the truth. It is ended." And thus, on the pavement of his little cell, singing "Glory be to the Father, and to the Son, and to the Holy Ghost," when he had named the Holy Ghost he breathed his last; and so departed to the heavenly kingdom, one whose name is the greatest in the ancient literature of Britain, and the most distinguished scholar of his age. I shall conclude this lecture with short extracts from two hymns composed by him in Latin, like most of his other works. The hymn from which the first extract is taken is entitled "Hymn for the Holy Innocents," and consists of six stanzas, the last of which is here given in the translation of John Mason Neale:—

> " O city [Bethlehem] blest o'er all the earth,
> Who gloriest in the Saviour's birth!
> Whose are his earliest martyrs dear,
> By kindred and by triumph here.
> None from henceforth may call thee small,—
> Of rival towns thou passest all,
> In whom our Monarch had his birth,
> O city blest o'er all the earth."

The following extract is from a hymn on the ascension of our Lord, translated by Elizabeth R. Charles:—

> " A hymn of glory let us sing;
> New songs throughout the world shall ring;
> By a new way none ever trod
> Christ mounteth to the throne of God.
>
> .   .   .   .   .   .
>
> May our affections thither tend,
> And thither constantly ascend,
> Where, seated on the Father's throne,
> Thee reigning in the heavens we own!
>
> Be thou our present joy, O Lord!
> Who wilt be ever our reward,
> And as the countless ages flee,
> May all our glory be in thee!"

SHORT LIST OF PUBLICATIONS

OF

JAMES GEMMELL,

10-15 GEORGE IV. BRIDGE,

EDINBURGH.

LONDON : . . . . . HAMILTON, ADAMS, & CO.; SIMPKIN, MARSHALL, & CO.
EDINBURGH : . . . . OLIVER & BOYD ; J. MENZIES & CO.
GLASGOW : . . . . , . . J. MENZIES & CO.; PORTEOUS BROTHERS.

THE ONLY HISTORY OF THE WESTMINSTER ASSEMBLY.

HISTORY OF THE WESTMINSTER ASSEMBLY OF DIVINES. By the late Wm. M. HETHERINGTON, D.D., LL.D., Free Church College, Glasgow. Edited by Dr Robert Williamson, Ascog. With Notes and Facsimiles of Title-Pages of the Original Editions of the Confession of Faith, the Catechisms, Larger and Shorter ; and the Directory for Church Government and Ordination of Ministers. Fourth Edition, in 1 vol., crown 8vo, cloth, price 6'.

"The value of the present edition has been greatly enhanced by the care and judgment with which Dr. Williamson of Ascog has readjusted its contents, and added what brings their information into accord with the light of the latest discoveries."—FREE CHURCH RECORD.

" Besides making such corrections as were rendered necessary by the publication of a portion of the Minutes above referred to, the editor has appended to this fourth edition a few additional notes, several facsimiles of seventeenth century title-pages, and two suitable and sufficient indices, additions which will considerably enhance the interest and value of the work."—SCOTSMAN.

IMPORTANT WORK ON DEFENCE OF CHURCH ESTABLISHMENTS.

STATEMENT BY THE LATE THOMAS M'CRIE, D.D., Author of "Life of John Knox," etc. With Preface by George Smeaton, D.D., Professor of Exegetical Theology, New College, Edinburgh. Crown 8vo, cloth, price 5/.

" It is a masterly defence of the Principle of Establishments as a Scripture Truth, and the most complete vindication ever given to the world of the position occupied by the Reformed Church of Scotland on the whole subject of National Religion, and of the magistrates' legitimate power in promoting it."—PREFACE BY PROFESSOR SMEATON.

"Apart from the editor's commendation, anything from the pen of so masculine a reasoner, and so well practised a writer as Dr. M'Crie must be worth reading ; and whoever wishes to study the important subject here treated of, will do well to have the little book beside him."—SCOTSMAN.

Now Ready, demy 8vo, cloth, price 9/.

HISTORY OF THE CANON OF THE HOLY SCRIPTURES IN THE CHRISTIAN CHURCH.

BY

EDWARD REUSS.

Professor in the University of Strasburg.

TRANSLATED BY

Rev. DAVID HUNTER, B.D.

"It is a book I highly value."—PROFESSOR BRUCE, Glasgow.
"The book is a most valuable and useful one."—PROFESSOR MILLIGAN, Aberdeen.
"I have long known the book, and found it very stimulating."—PROFESSOR CHARTERIS, Edinburgh.
"The work of M. Reuss, the venerable theologian of Strasburg, on the History of the Canon, has all the merits of careful research, comprehension, grasp, and lucid exposition, that mark his other well-known writings, while it has also the special merit of handling the subject from a standpoint sufficiently different from the other writers who have dealt with it, to give to his book a peculiar and, in some sense, unique value, and to make the possession of it indispensable to the student who would acquaint himself with the various aspects of the questions discussed. Mr. Hunter has performed a signal service by making it accessible to the English reader in a version which I cannot doubt, from my knowledge of his qualifications, will contrast favourably with many translations of theological works, alike as regards accuracy and idiomatic clearness of rendering."—PROF. DICKSON, Glasgow.
"The subject is in itself interesting, and has a special interest for Scotsmen in view of recent controversies. The book is pleasantly written and very readable, and that is something to which on these subjects we are not accustomed. The style and treatment are luminous throughout. The spirit and method are strictly scientific. The interest, so to speak, is maintained from the beginning, but gathers chiefly around the closing chapters."—DUNDEE ADVERTISER
"The book ought to be in the library of every clergyman and theological student, and indeed will prove invaluable to every thoughtful reader who takes an interest in a subject of such vast importance."—BOOKSELLER.
"A most scholarly and comprehensive work. The most complete on the subject we know of."—CHRISTIAN AGE.
"In translating this book the Rev. David Hunter has done good service to theology, placing within the reach of all English readers what is now regarded as the most complete and most scholarly history of the canon yet written. The aim of the work is to show how the canon of Scripture we now possess came to include so many books, why not more or less. The book is neither critical nor dogmatic, but historical throughout. It is simply a record of facts left to speak for themselves. The author perceiving a gradual growth in the history of the canon, strives to make this development clear to others. Wide knowledge of Church history, impartial judgment of the evidence of facts, keen historical insight are certainly not lacking in the "History of the Canon." As a translation, we find everywhere good, idiomatic English, while its accuracy is guaranteed by the fact that all the proof-sheets have been revised by the author himself." LITERARY WORLD.
"We are glad that at last the reproach of this country is being removed, and that in so excellent and accurate a translation as this by Mr. Hunter, which has received the author's revision, English readers are enabled to find one of the very best, most unbiassed, and distinctly scientific works upon the Canon."—SCOTSMAN.

Crown 8vo, cloth, price 4/6.

MODERN MISSIONS AND CULTURE;
THEIR MUTUAL RELATIONS.

BY

Dr. GUSTAV WARNECK,

PASTOR AT ROTHENSCHIRMBACH, NEAR EISLEBEN.

Translated from the German by

THOMAS SMITH, D.D.,

PROFESSOR OF EVANGELISTIC THEOLOGY, NEW COLLEGE, EDINBURGH.

" What the author has done, is the vindication of missionaries from many baseless charges, and the proof that, among many failures, missions have wrought lasting and most important beneficial results. Sensible, and far from uninteresting."—SCOTSMAN.

" In the translator's excellent introduction to the work, special reference is made to Mr. Henry Stanley Newman, who went to India a few months ago, mainly with the view of visiting the missions of his own body, the Society of Friends. Dr. Smith has performed an eminently seasonable task in translating the book of the good German pastor, which contains a vast amount of well-digested and trustworthy information, all tending to confirm the belief that, among the culture forces of the world, Christianity is the most intrinsic, the most fundamental, and the most inspiriting."—NORTH BRITISH DAILY MAIL.

" Those interested in Foreign Missionary Works will be pleased with this book, since it aims at promoting greater unity on the part of so-called Christian people. The translator, while accepting the conclusions of the German Doctor, as 'sound and convincing,' vigorously answers some disparaging remarks passed on the educational method of conducting missions, a system very successfully applied in India by the late Dr. Duff."—DAILY CHRONICLE.

" Dr. Thomas Smith was a valued co-adjutor of Dr. Duff in Indian Mission Work, and in a preface to ' Modern Missions and Culture,' states that he had contemplated writing a book upon Missionary Enterprise. After, however, reading Dr. Warneck's treatise, he saw that his object would be attained in translating it. Dr. Warneck elaborately discusses mission work in all its bearings. The book is full of instructive facts and criticisms, and should be carefully studied by the members of our Churches."—DUNDEE ADVERTISER.

" This is a most fascinating volume. From the first page to the last it sustains the reader's interest, and gives an admirable account of the relations of Missions and Culture. No such important missionary volume has been issued in recent years. We were specially impressed by the judicial spirit which reigns throughout it, and the admirable good sense which characterises many of its remarks. Dr. Smith has done his part of the work with great faithfulness."—PRESBYTERIAN CHURCHMAN.

" Professor Smith has done a great service in introducing Dr. Warneck's book to the English reader. In days when we have so-called culture set even above the Gospel, it is well to have it thoroughly discussed, and shown that there can be no morality without religion, and that Christianity is chief among the culture forces of the world. This is what Dr. Warneck has done. But he has done a great deal more : he has surveyed the mission-field, he has noticed the objections against missions to the heathen that crop up every now and then in the unbelieving press, he examines them and shows their baselessness. It is, therefore, a book for the times, and will be read with interest and profit by the multitudes of good people who desire to see heathenism speedily take its place among the things of the past, and who believe Christianity to be the divinely appointed means for bringing about the achievement."—CHRISTIAN TREASURY.

" Shows, by the statement of interesting facts, the great influence of missions in the successful promotion of the educational progress, and the civilisation of heathen countries."—DUNDEE COURIER.

Demy 8vo, cloth, with Illustrations, price 7/6.

LECTURES AND SERMONS

BY

MARTYRS.

CONTAINING SERMONS AND LECTURES BY

RICHARD CAMERON.	ALEXANDER SHIELDS.
ALEXANDER PEDEN.	JOHN LIVINGSTONE.
DONALD CARGILL.	JOHN WELLWOOD.
WILLIAM GUTHRIE.	JOHN WELSH.
MICHAEL BRUCE.	JOHN GUTHRIE.

With Preface by JOHN HOWIE, of Lochgoin; and Brief Biographical Notices of the Authors of the Sermons, by the Rev. JAMES KERR, Glasgow.

ILLUSTRATIONS.—Grassmarket of Edinburgh—Canongate Tolbooth—Martyrs' Monument, Greyfriars—The House where Cameron was born—Netherbow Port, Edinburgh—Greyfriars' Churchyard—Monument at Airsmoss—Bothwell Bridge.

"'These sermons were first published by the celebrated John Howie, of Lochgoin, in 1779. This edition having long since become very scarce, if obtainable at all, it was a good thought to have it reprinted. This has been done under the careful editorship of the Rev. James Kerr, of Greenock. . . . No one that values the contendings of Scotland's martyrs should be without a copy."—COVENANTER.

"This volume is fitted to prove a genuine memorial of the humble, yet truly illustrious band who jeoparded their lives for Christ's crown and the nation's weal. . . . . The book is altogether very creditably got up, and extends to 674 pages of closely printed matter."—R. P. WITNESS.

THE TRUE PSALMODY; The Bible Psalms the Church's only Manual of Praise. With Prefaces by the Rev. Drs Cooke, Edgar, and Houston, and Recommendations from Eminent Presbyterian Divines. Crown 8vo, cloth, 220 pages, price 2/.

"The 'True Psalmody,' is a book that is calculated, we firmly believe, to convince any mind that is open to conviction, that the use of hymns is wholly unwarrantable. It is seldom in these days of 'liberal views' that is, of wholesale corruption of doctrine and worship—that we meet with a new publication that we heartily and unreservedly commend." THE REFORMED PRESBYTERIAN WITNESS.

SELECT SERMONS BY THOMAS CHALMERS, D.D., LL.D. With a Tribute to his Memory by the late Dr. LORIMER. New edition, crown 8vo, cloth, 233 pages, price 1 6.

"Judiciously selected, and will serve, as far as printed words can serve, to convey to a new generation an idea of the power and eloquence which entranced their fathers. It is fitting, too, that Dr. Lorimer's funeral sermon should escape any hostile criticism. From an evangelical and Free Church point of view, the sermon is a noble eloge."—SCOTSMAN.

Demy 8vo, cloth, in 2 vols., price 3/6 each vol. (sold separately).

MODERN SCOTTISH PULPIT.

CONTAINING

SERMONS BY PRESBYTERIAN MINISTERS.

"There are weighty doctrinal discourses, scholarly expositions of Scripture, ably maintained theses, pointed practical exhortations, and fervent evangelical appeals. . . . . They possess all the characteristics of what has been known as distinctly Scottish preaching."—DAILY REVIEW.

"*Scotch Sermons* are not all bad, though the name has gained an unenviable notoriety ; for here are discourses 'as sound as a bell.' Sydney Smith called Scotland 'the knuckle-end of England ;' but as to gospel preaching we have always regarded it as the choicest part of the three kingdoms ; and so it is, and so shall be, by the grace of God."—REV. C. H. SPURGEON.

"Presents excellent specimens of the modern evangelical preaching at its best."—LIVERPOOL MERCURY.

"These sermons represent the talent of the living Church in every part of the country."—PERTHSHIRE CONSTITUTIONAL.

"One and all of them, we believe, give forth a certain sound on the great verities of the gospel."—ORIGINAL SECESSION MAGAZINE.

WORKS BY REV. HUGH MARTIN, D.D.

THE ATONEMENT ; in its Relation to the Priesthood and the Intercession of our Lord. 2nd edition, demy 8vo, cloth, price 7/6.

"A volume written with remarkable vigour and earnestness."—BRITISH QUARTERLY REVIEW.

"Something like theology. We wish our young divines would feed on such meat as this. Dr. Martin teaches a real substitution and an efficient atonement, and has no sympathy with Robertson and his school."—SPURGEON.

THE SHADOW OF CALVARY : Gethsemane—The Arrest—The Trial. Demy 8vo, cloth, price 7/6.

"We recommend the 'Shadow of Calvary' to our readers,as an excellent book for Sabbath reading, and we trust it will have a large circulation. It abounds in close heart-searching appeals to the unbelieving and impenitent and with rich consolations to the humble child of God. —THE ORIGINAL SECESSION MAGAZINE.

"It will be seen that Dr. Martin holds very definite theological views, and that he is neither afraid nor ashamed to proclaim them. . . . These lectures abounding in powerful appeal and stern warnings, are not deficient in tenderness and reverence."—SCOTSMAN.

THE PROPHET JONAH : his Character and Mission to Nineveh. 2nd edition, demy 8vo, price 7/6

"To ordinary readers we can thoroughly recommend it as a good, sound, full, practical exposition of the Prophet Jonah."—DAILY REVIEW.

"A good specimen of the author's power of exposition, and is certain to be useful to those who intend to devote special study to the book."—GLASGOW NEWS.

A METHOD OF PRAYER, with Scripture Expressions Proper to be Used under each Head. By the late Rev. MATTHEW HENRY. 16mo, cloth, price 1/.

THE SAINTS EVERLASTING REST ; or, a Treatise on the Blessed State of the Saints in their Enjoyment of God in Heaven. By the Rev. Richard Baxter. Abridged by Benjamin Fawcett, M.A. New edition, 12mo, cloth, price 1 6.

IMPORTANT WORK ON BAPTISM. [*Originally published in 1791.*]

CANDID REASONS FOR RENOUNCING THE PRINCIPLES OF ANTIPÆDOBAPTISM. By Peter Edwards. Crown 8vo, cloth, price 2 6.

With NOTE recommending it by—Principals Rainy and Douglas ; Professors M'Gregor, Thos. Smith and Smeaton ; Drs. H. Bonar, Kennedy, Wilson, and Begg. Principal Lindsay Alexander, Dr. James M'Gregor, St. Cuthbert's, Edinburgh ; and Dr. Robert Jamieson, St. Paul's, Glasgow.

Crown 8vo, 357 pages, price 4 6.

THE STORY OF DANIEL:
HIS LIFE AND TIMES.
BY
P. H. HUNTER,
MINISTER OF ELIE.

"The book is a graphic and vigorous historical biography, as engrossing as a volume of Macaulay."—SCOTSMAN.

"Mr. Hunter has done his work very thoroughly. . . . . His volume will occupy a place which there has hitherto been no English book to fill."—THE GLASGOW HERALD.

Just Ready, fcap. 8vo, price 1 6.

OUR MOTHER:
A LIFE PICTURE.
BEING A LIFE OF MRS. KRUMMACHER,
WIFE OF THE AUTHOR OF "THE SUFFERING SAVIOUR," ETC.

Translated from the German by a well-known Author.

"Deep appreciation of the purity and peace of home-life enables German writers to depict it as no others can. . . . . Possesses all the pathos, sweet simplicity, and lofty teaching which characterise the best German story writers The translation is beautifully done. A capital gift-book."—IRISH BAPTIST MAGAZINE.

THE CROOK IN THE LOT; OR, THE SOVEREIGNTY AND WISDOM OF GOD IN THE AFFLICTIONS OF MEN DISPLAYED ; together with a Christian Deportment under them : being the Substance of several Sermons on Eccles. vii. 13, Prov. xvi. 17, and 1 Pet. v. 6. By Rev. Thomas Boston. 16mo, cloth, price 8d.

Crown 8vo, cloth, 178 pages, with portrait, price 3/.

LIFE
OF

ROBERT SMITH CANDLISH, D.D.,
MINISTER OF FREE ST. GEORGE'S CHURCH, AND PRINCIPAL OF THE
NEW COLLEGE, EDINBURGH.

By JEAN L. WATSON.

"A most admirable sketch of the character and work of the late Dr Candlish. . . . . This is a most seasonable publication, and should be read by all who want to get a concise and coprehensive account of the important principles and controversies with which Dr. Candlish was so much identified."—DAILY REVIEW.

"In selection, arrangement, and graphic description, the little volume is all that could be desired."—EDINBURGH COURANT.

"Many will rejoice in the opportunity of possessing the smaller and cheaper life of the great leader, now published, who could not spare the price of the former one. And they will find all the leading events of a remarkable career of one of the most eminent men the Church has ever had recorded in the volume now before us, with a fidelity, sympathy, and brevity that are really very pleasing."—INVERNESS ADVERTISER.

Crown 8vo, cloth, price 2/.

LIFE AND TIMES
OF

THOMAS BOSTON:
PASTOR OF ETTRICK.

By JEAN L. WATSON.

"That the autobiography is so little known is much to be regretted; it is a picture of one of the most momentous periods in the religious history of Scotland; it is moreover, the mirror of a life spent in high communion with God, and gifted with a vision penetrating far into the kingdom. Miss Watson's "Life" is based upon this larger work, and abundant extracts are given from it. She has selected her materials wisely, and the result is a book which cannot fail to interest."—BRITISH MESSENGER.

Just published, crown 8vo, cloth, price 1.6.

THE LIFE
OF

ANDREW THOMSON, D.D.

By JEAN L. WATSON.

"Her biography will be prized."—SCOTSMAN.

"This interesting but all too brief memoir of Dr. Andrew Thomson will do much to supply a long felt want. Considering the scanty materials she had to work with, Miss Watson has succeeded in giving us a really valuable and much needed sketch of the life and labours of one of the greatest preachers of this country. . . . . The chapter of 'Personal Reminiscences,' by the Rev. Wm. Cousin, greatly enhances the value of the volume."—DAILY REVIEW.

"The compiler of a brief life of the well-known Dr. Andrew Thomson has done her work with conscientious care evidently, ... will be found of interest to many as a record of the life of a very able, manly, and large-hearted Christian minister."—ABERDEEN FREE PRESS.

OUR CHILDREN FOR CHRIST; A PLEA FOR INFANT

CHURCH MEMBERSHIP, with a full Discussion of the Mode of Baptism. By Rev. SAMUEL MACNAUGHTON, M.A., English Presbyterian Church, Preston. 12mo, cloth, price 9d.

"Free from all controversial bitterness."—DAILY REVIEW.
"These arguments will no doubt be regarded as convincing by the numerous sections of the Christian Church who accept the doctrine." SCOTSMAN.
"The book is one of marked ability. In our opinion irresistible."—THE CHRISTIAN NEWS.

Cr. 8vo, cloth, 203 pp., with Two Portraits and Engraving of Gairney Bridge. Price 1s 6d.

THE ERSKINES:

EBENEZER AND RALPH.

BY

JOHN KER, D.D., AND JEAN L. WATSON.

"A better prize book for a U.P. Sabbath school could not be found. The story of the lives of Ebenezer and Ralph Erskine here told is full of interest. But its power to engage attention is not its only virtue. It shows the manner of men the founders of the denomination were—how intensely earnest and practical their religion was; how *sincer* their attachment to principle, how manifest their labours, and how lofty their aims; and it therefore commands admiration as well as excites interest."—DAILY REVIEW.
"This is the joint-production of a distinguished U.P. divine and a well-known Free Church authoress. They have succeeded between them in making a very readable book, ... is written in an agreeable and attractive style, which is certain to ensure its popularity."—EDINBURGH COURANT.

BY JEAN L. WATSON.

LIFE OF RICHARD CAMERON. 70 pp., with View of Monument at Airsmoss, and of Falkland Palace, price 6d.

"Miss Watson still continues her praiseworthy efforts to supply lives of 'Scottish Worthies' calculated to instruct youthful readers and stimulate them to useful and holy lives. . . . . Contains a brief and appreciative biography of Richard Cameron, and a graphic account of the persecutions he endured during the memorable covenanting struggle."—EDINBURGH COURANT.

LIFE OF HUGH MILLER. 132 pp., with View of Bass Rock on cover, price 9d.

"This is a well-condensed biographical notice of Hugh Miller, stonemason, geologist, and editor."—DAILY REVIEW.
"Gives on the whole a fair and just view of the salient features of his character."—ABERDEEN FREE PRESS.

LIFE OF THOMAS CHALMERS, D.D., LL.D. With View of Kilmany Church. 134 pp., price 9d.

"The picture she presents of the great Free Churchman is, we believe, essentially just and true, as it certainly is attractive." DAILY REVIEW.
"Skilfully selected, the crowning incidents of his life, and some of the descriptions rise to eloquence."—LEAGUE JOURNAL.